Studying at University

Studying at University is an essential guide for anyone wanting to know how they can make the very best of their university experience. This down-to-earth book offers guidance to those in sixth form and college on what universities are all about and what being a student actually involves. The author also offers straightforward advice to new and existing students on how they should set about their studies.

Key topics include:

- choosing the university that is best for you
- preparing yourself for university life
- how and why universities are so different from school
- how to get the most out of lectures, seminars and tutorials
- preparing and writing essays and assignments
- revising for exams and exam technique.

Written by a university lecturer with vast experience of speaking to students about this nerve-wracking process, this engaging and accessible book is an indispensable companion for anyone who wants their move into higher education to be as informed and stress-free as possible.

G.W. Bernard is Reader in History at the University of Southampton.

Studying at University

How to adapt successfully to college life

G.W. Bernard

Routledge
Taylor & Francis Group

LONDON AND NEW YORK

First published 2003 by Routledge
11 New Fetter Lane, London EC4P 4EE

Simultaneously published in the USA and Canada
by Routledge
29 West 35th Street, New York, NY 10001

Routledge is an imprint of the Taylor & Francis Group

Typeset in Goudy by GreenGate Publishing Services, Tonbridge, Kent
Printed and bound in Great Britain by TJ International Ltd, Padstow,
Cornwall

British Library Cataloguing in Publication Data
A catalogue record for this book is available from the British Library

Library in Congress Cataloging-in-Publication Data
A catalog record for this book has been requested

ISBN 0-415-30311-7 (HB)
ISBN 0-415-30312-5 (PB)

Contents

Preface

I have written this book above all as a manual for students. First, I offer guidance to those in sixth forms and colleges who are thinking about applying to university and want to know more about university life. My book sketches what modern universities are about and what being a student involves. Secondly, and partly as a way of achieving its first aim, my book offers advice to new and existing students on how they should set about their studies. It is thus a book to be referred to again and again over the years of sixth form and university study.

I hope that this book will also be of value to three further audiences. Many parents have little personal experience of universities, while the great changes that have taken place in the past decade mean that even those who are themselves graduates risk being out of touch with recent developments. Sixth-form teachers who advise prospective students on university entry and who are developing their teaching as a bridge between school and university study will, I hope, find my account of what is happening in higher education useful. And university lecturers who are increasingly being called upon explicitly to teach study skills to their students in formal courses may find this book helpful in preparing such teaching.

There are, of course, many books of advice for students. This one differs for three reasons. First, it is written not by a professional educational adviser or psychologist, but by an historian who for twenty-five years has been teaching in higher education, first at what was then a polytechnic, and then at an old university. It thus reflects my experience of teaching a demanding subject, rather than contrived experiments or explorations in theory. Secondly, it offers both an idealistic defence of university study at its best and a realistic assessment of what being a student means in practice in a world of underfunding. It shows what students can achieve but it also describes realities. Thirdly, it reflects my experience as an historian in that I believe firmly that students will study better and have a greater understanding of what they are about if they have some sense of the history – or background – of universities and of the current context, political, financial and social, in which universities find themselves.

My experience as an historian means that this book will doubtless be most valuable for those thinking of studying history and subjects in the humanities and social sciences. But while I have drawn on my experience and in places chosen historical examples to illustrate my points, those points are intended to have more general significance. And students of different subjects can usefully reflect on what it is that makes their subject different.

Anyone offering such advice risks the charge of arrogance. It is easy to give offence, particularly since in print such advice often reads not as a possibly useful suggestion – something that you might benefit from thinking about – but rather as a set of barked instructions. Despite that danger, I have deliberately set out my points boldly so that they are clear. But I must emphasise that there are no golden rules, no magical formulae that guarantee success. Ultimately my justification here is that everyone can profit from thinking about how they are studying, and this book should best be seen as a contribution to such reflection.

This book is set out in three parts. Of course, like all authors, I should be pleased if you read right through my book. But this book has deliberately been organised so that you can read what is most relevant to your immediate concerns. My advice on how to study fills the second half of the book. If what you want is guidance on how to write essays or how to prepare for examinations, go straight to the chapters on those topics. The earlier chapters are intended to give you information on what universities are about, something that will be especially helpful to those who are choosing a university. I believe it is helpful, whatever you are considering, to know something about its past. So the very first part of my book sketches how universities began and how they have come to be what they are now. But you do not have to start there: go to whatever is of most importance to you.

Acknowledgements

Let me explain how I came to write this book and thank those friends who have helped me. One recent summer my colleague Neil Gregor, admissions tutor, asked for volunteers to respond to an invitation from St Bartholomew's School, Newbury, for a lecturer from the Department of History at Southampton to talk to their sixth form. I volunteered in the belief that what they wanted was a talk on an historical subject, and I offered to speak on my special interest, the reign of Henry VIII. But ten days before I was due to speak, it turned out that what they wanted was a talk on studying at university to be given to some 200 lower-sixth-formers. It was too late to turn back, so I set down some thoughts, based on what over the years I have been advising generations of my students, and duly gave a 45-minute talk. Ten days later, waiting for a train at Reading Station, a young man came up to me, introduced himself as one of my audience that day, and said how interesting he had found my lecture. Around that time I happened to see a fellow rail passenger engrossed in a book called something like 'How to Study at University'. And so it occurred to me that I might try to enlarge and publish what I had prepared for my talk. What turned such vague inclinations into what you see here was the subsequent extended Christmas and New Year holiday. Frustrated that I could not for nearly two weeks go into my office or study in a library or a record office, I set to work on the computer at home, and in that time, plus the following weekend and a couple of evenings after that, I had written a draft of this book. I must thank a number of friends for their comments and encouragement: Neil Gregor, Mark Stoyle and Alastair Duke at Southampton, John Benson and Harvey Woolf at Wolverhampton; Greg Walker at Leicester; John Hall at King Edward VI School, Southampton; Anne Borg at Oxford.

If you have any comments or suggestions I should be delighted to hear from you.

Part I

How universities began

Chapter 1

Beginnings and developments

As an historian, I always find it helpful in considering a new subject not simply to look at what there is now, but to find out how what is there now came to be there. We may not always like what we inherit from the past, and we are particularly likely to reject our most immediate inheritance, but if we wish to understand, and more especially if we wish to reform, the institutions and practices with which we have grown up, then it is essential to know how they have come to be what they are now. There is a temptation to think that what exists has always existed: it can be a shock to realise that some things have not been as they are now for very long. Often the name or description remains unchanged over a long period, but the realities it represents are very different. In this part of my book I give a brief sketch of how universities have come to be as they are now. I think that knowing a little of this background will be useful for you. But you do not have to begin here – go directly to the next chapter, or to the advice in Part III, if you wish.

Universities are one of the oldest and most characteristic institutions of Western society, but they have changed considerably over time, and, not least, in the last ten years. They have not always existed. In ancient Greece and Rome, great civilisations though they were, lasting several centuries, there were no universities. No oriental or Muslim civilisation developed anything like a university. In all these societies there were, of course, scholars, men – almost always men – who devoted themselves to study, but it was not until the twelfth century AD that anything that is recognisable as a university emerged anywhere. It is then – a century after the Norman Conquest of England in 1066 – that in Italy, in France and in England we find the first universities.

Before that, institutions of the Christian church, especially cathedrals (the principal church in the diocese of a bishop) and monasteries (where small groups of men who had taken a vow of celibacy spent their lives performing a rigorous round of daily services) often developed schools. Some of the clergy and monks would concentrate on teaching young boys. Much of that teaching was basic instruction, but in some places and at some times it went rather further. Some of the teachers were learned men in their own right. And some of the monks were simply scholars. Such schools acquired reputations as centres of learning. Young scholars would travel from England to northern France and to Italy in pursuit of their studies.

What seems to have happened in the twelfth century is that many such scholars and teachers found the monastic rule – the need to perform several services daily – increasingly burdensome. They may simply have been so excited by their studies that they wanted to devote themselves entirely to them. They may also have wished to study and to teach subjects such as medicine that did not fit easily into the life of a monastery. They may have wished to be free from the daily control of a bishop or an abbot: we can only speculate, since there are no statements of intent, no manifestos, no interviews. But we do know that many scholars and learned men formed themselves into a group – or society, or gild, or, to use the word that caught on, a *universitas* – of 'masters', or scholars, who organised the study of young men willing to pay for such guidance.

The key feature was that these studies were organised. It was not a matter of dropping by to hear a lecture, or of living in a scholar's household for a while and engaging in dialogue. Buildings were set aside or constructed specially for the purpose of teaching and of study. Constitutions spelled out how the university was organised. The teachers were grouped together by subjects: and these groupings were called faculties or (confusingly for the modern student) schools. Formal syllabuses were set down, stating what needed to be studied, and over what period of time. Schemes of assessment tested whether students had succeeded. And then these societies of scholars obtained recognition from existing authorities, above all from the church: licences were granted by the pope allowing these universities to award certificates – or degrees – to those who had successfully completed their studies.

A typical medieval student might start aged fourteen and spend a year each studying grammar, rhetoric and logic, taught in the Faculty of Arts, after which he would become a Bachelor of Arts; he would then spend a year each studying arithmetic, geometry, music and astronomy, leading, after a total of seven years, to the degree of Master of Arts. A successful MA might then undertake advanced study in the Faculties of Theology or Canon Law, or Civil Law or Medicine. That would be rewarded by the degree of Doctor. The word 'doctor' is derived from the Latin *doceo*, meaning 'I teach'. Once you had achieved a doctorate, you were deemed qualified to teach students yourself.

Recognisable here are the foundations of the modern university. Evidently there were significant numbers of young men who wanted to study and who could afford to do so. Their studies were organised and formalised. Their teachers were grouped together in forerunners of modern university subject departments. And the emergence of universities reflects wider economic developments in Western European society – part of the so-called 'twelfth century Renaissance'. Another important factor was the significant growth in the scale of government and administration in the twelfth century: there was consequently an increased demand for well-educated administrators in church and state.

Encyclopedias and guide books will give you more or less precise dates at which the earliest universities were 'founded' – Bologna, in Italy, in 1158, Paris around 1175, Oxford around 1188. But that is misleading. Nowadays it is quite feasible for a government to announce that it will found a university in a place where there was no university before, and then go ahead and create it by an act of will. That was not how universities began. Bologna, Paris and Oxford were clearly recognised centres of study before the teachers there formed themselves into gilds recognised as universities by various kinds of charters from kings and popes. But once universities had emerged and been recognised as such, it was then possible for the model to be imitated: new universities were set up in France, in Italy, and later in Germany and other countries.

In England, two universities emerged: first Oxford in the late twelfth century and then, early in the thirteenth, Cambridge. They became unusual in European terms in the development not just of buildings in which lectures were given and hostels or halls in which advanced students lived, but also colleges as corporate bodies employing teachers, or Fellows as they were called, and so combining teaching and accommodation. The earliest colleges were designed for the teachers and for the most advanced students; in time they came to include younger students as well; and over the centuries the halls or hostels were absorbed by or turned into colleges. New colleges were founded from time to time, by grants of land from kings, queens, churchmen (such as William, archdeacon of Durham, who in 1249 left money which led to the emergence of University College, Oxford, or Walter of Merton, who endowed Merton College in 1264), and landowners (such as John de Balliol who endowed what later became the college named after him at

Oxford 1263–68). William of Wykeham's New College, Oxford (1379) set the pattern of colleges controlling the teaching of undergraduates. By the middle of the seventeenth century most of the colleges of Oxford and Cambridge had come into being.

The curriculum changed, with some striking developments, in the sixteenth century. The syllabus sketched above yielded to intense study of selected Latin and Greek texts, with an emphasis on rhetoric and language. The system of what at Oxford are called Honour Schools – studying a set subject or group of subjects and taking examinations at the end of three or four years – was established in the early nineteenth century. *Literae Humaniores* (ancient history, classical languages and literature and philosophy) was the most popular until it was displaced by Modern History at the end of the nineteenth century. Science and engineering rose significantly then.

By European standards, England had astonishingly few universities. Until 1827 there were only two – Oxford and Cambridge. By contrast Scotland, an independent country until 1603, but with a much smaller population than England, had St Andrews, Glasgow and Aberdeen in the fifteenth century, Edinburgh from 1583, and a second university in Aberdeen (Marischal College) from 1593. Not until the early nineteenth century were more universities established in England. University College, London, was founded in 1827, King's College, London, in 1829, followed by several more colleges in London – Imperial, Bedford, Queen Mary, and the London School of Economics. The university of Durham was endowed by the bishop of Durham in 1832. The universities of the great industrial and commercial cities of the North and Midlands were founded from the middle of the century, usually on the initiative of local industrialists or businessmen, with royal charters marking successful development: Manchester 1851 (and granted a charter in 1880), Leeds 1874 (charter in 1904), Bristol 1876 (charter in 1909), Birmingham 1880 (charter in 1898), Liverpool 1881 (charter in 1901), Reading 1892 (charter in 1925), Sheffield 1897 (charter in 1905). In Wales Aberystwyth, Bangor, and Cardiff came in 1893, Swansea in 1920. A new development was the emergence of university colleges under the authority of the University of London whose external degrees they awarded: Nottingham, Southampton, Leicester, Exeter and Hull. In time these too were granted royal charters. All of these had followed a similar pattern and were collectively styled 'redbrick' universities – many of their late Victorian buildings were built with red bricks – or 'civic' or (less flatteringly) 'provincial' universities. Outside Stoke-on-Trent, at Keele, a rather different pattern – a four-year degree with a common first-year, now abandoned – was followed in the establishment of what became the University of Keele (1950).

Parallel to the foundation of new universities were two further important educational developments. Training colleges were set up to train teachers for primary schools. The first emerged from a school to teach the children of the poor set up in Southwark by an eccentric Quaker, Joseph Lancaster in 1798, which developed into the Borough Road Teacher Training College. In 1838 the Church of England, which through various bodies had supported charity schools, resolved that it was no longer sufficient for teachers to learn their craft simply by serving as apprentices to existing teachers; they needed more formal training. The College of St Mark's, later the College of St Mark and St John, was set up in Chelsea, London, on the model (but lacking the endowments) of Oxford and Cambridge colleges. By mid-century there were over twenty teacher training colleges, other religious denominations followed suit, and a national body was set up to oversee them and lay down syllabuses and examinations. In the early twentieth century a number of cities established their own teacher training colleges, notably Leeds. There was also a substantial growth of local technical colleges for technical vocational training, especially from the late nineteenth century. Neither training colleges nor technical colleges were universities, but sometimes they had links with universities, particularly in the case of the training colleges. From the 1890s many universities set up departments of education, offering courses that combined the practical training in training colleges with more academic studies; many of these university departments took on the task of validating – for example, by setting and marking examination papers – the qualifications offered in training colleges.

There was then a new wave of expansion of universities in the early 1960s – Sussex, York, Warwick, Kent, Lancaster, Essex, and the colleges of advanced technology, Brunel, Bath and Aston. It was an expansion justified by the famous Robbins report of 1963. In the mid-1960s Tony Crosland, then Labour Minister of Education, decided that further expansion in what was increasingly being called 'higher education' would be achieved by renaming some thirty of the existing technical colleges as 'polytechnics', and allowing them to prepare students for BA or BSc degrees, initially under the umbrella of the Council for National Academic Awards. In the 1970s many of these absorbed some of the earlier teacher training colleges. In 1992 these polytechnics were allowed to call themselves universities and granted royal charters permitting them to award their own degrees. A number of former teacher training colleges, which had earlier been renamed colleges of higher education, increased in size, and permitted to offer degree courses, were also allowed to call themselves universities (or sometimes 'university sector colleges', meaning that the degrees they award are validated by another university).

That sketch of developments must be supplemented by looking at numbers. The earliest universities were very small – at best a few hundred students. As recently as just before the Second World War, there were only 50,000 full-time students in the UK. Writing just after the end of the war, Bruce Truscot commented on the proposals of the National Union of Students – 'which habitually goes to enthusiastic extremes' – that the university population should rise to 200,000 or 250,000: 'if England, instead of twelve universities totalling (before the War) 35,000 students, had sixteen with an average of 3000 each, all reasonable demands would be met for a long time to come'. (Adding in the universities in the rest of the UK would have pushed Truscot's optimum number up to 60,000.) By 1960 there were 200,000 students, approaching the NUS's 'enthusiastic extreme of 1945'; by 1968 this had risen to 400,000, and by 1990 to 600,000. Now there are nearly 1,500,000. There are now more students in Newcastle-upon-Tyne and Sunderland combined – some 54,000 – than there were in the whole of the United Kingdom on the eve of the Second World War. What is called the 'participation rate', the number of students as a proportion of the total number of 18–21-year-olds, has shot up: one in twelve at universities (plus one in twelve at what were then technical colleges and became polytechnics) when I was a student in the late 1960s; now well over one in three (and approaching two in five); Mr Tony Blair, the Prime Minister, speaks of moving to one in two, and this was indeed a formal election manifesto commitment in 2001.

That increase in student numbers is a staggering social and educational change. Much, though far from all of it, reflects the entry of women into higher education. Until the late nineteenth century, only men went to university. The first women's colleges were Girton (1869) and Newnham (1872) in Cambridge, then Lady Margaret Hall (1879) and Somerville (1879) in Oxford, but until 1920 at Oxford and 1948 in Cambridge women were not formally allowed to take degrees. As late as 1960 of the 200,000 students only a quarter were women. That ratio has now been transformed. Anyone looking back at that can only be astonished that it took so long.

Moreover until the late nineteenth century virtually all university students were not only men, but adolescent men. In medieval universities, the age of entry could be as young as 14 or 15; the current typical age of 18 is a late nineteenth-century development. Birkbeck College, whose origins lay in an early nineteenth-century mechanics' institute, was incorporated into the University of London in 1858, its role to offer a university education to older and employed students, with all teaching taking place in the evenings. From the 1920s the University of London offered external degrees for which students could study by correspondence, again aimed at older students in employment. And with the development of the polytechnics, now the new universities, and then the training colleges in the 1970s, came a greater emphasis on mature students. Other universities responded by also accepting as students men and women who were older than the traditional norm of 18. These 'mature students' now make up a significant proportion of the total student population, especially in the new universities, in some of which more than half the students are 'mature'.

Part II

What universities are about

Chapter 2

What makes universities special?

So what is the point, what is the benefit, of going to university? Quite simply, it is greatly enriching to continue studying beyond A levels. If you are now a sixth-former, think of yourself as you were, say, two years ago, and consider how much you have learned, how much your abilities have developed since then. What makes the years of late adolescence so fruitful is that this period in life offers the optimum combination of the energy and openness to new ideas characteristic of youth on the one hand with a now already solid base of learning and maturity on the other. It is not an accident that it is those aged 18–21 that provide the largest category by far of the country's university students.

But why go to a university in order to continue studying? Why not stay on at school? What is the difference between university and school? The difference is that those who teach in universities are also engaged in research, and it is this that makes them such rewarding places to study in.

Schoolteachers are not expected to research, nor are they given the time to do so. Think how many classes a schoolteacher takes each week; think how many different aspects of a subject a schoolteacher teaches. A history master might teach twentieth-century history at GCSE, sixteenth-century history to the junior classes and nineteenth-century history to the seniors. Schoolteachers teach at many different levels, from A level to 11–13-year-olds: these different groups require very different approaches. Schoolteachers also often have to teach pupils of widely varying abilities and to cope with very different levels of commitment to study, not to mention the most basic challenge of maintaining order. So what schoolteachers have to do is to 'get up' their subjects (including many which they have not had the time to study for any great length of time or in any depth, and on which they are therefore unlikely to be able to say anything original), to adjust and simplify them according to the age and abilities of their pupils, which obviously is especially necessary for younger pupils, and then to stimulate and discipline them into learning.

University lecturers by contrast teach students over 18, that is to say individuals who are adults, and who are at university from their own choice (not because they are compelled to by law), having secured A-level passes showing that they have attained a certain level of competence (or, if they are mature students who have not obtained such formal certificates of attainment, are by definition highly motivated). For the lecturers that means that to a large extent they can teach on their own terms, without having to worry about discipline, and without having to simplify greatly.

University teachers teach perhaps ten hours a week on average for some 24–30 weeks of the year (though there are quite considerable variations between universities). That means that they have time (if rather less than was once the case) to get on with research (as we shall soon consider more fully). They teach a much more restricted range of topics within their subject than schoolteachers do. For example, all my teaching is concentrated on sixteenth- and seventeenth-century history, mainly English history, and such concentration of teaching on broadly defined areas of research interest is characteristic. Compared with schoolteachers, university lecturers do not have to spread themselves too thinly – although in some less well funded universities, lecturers are under greater pressure to do just that, as we shall see.

How did we become university teachers? We began as students ourselves, studying for BA or BSc degrees. Then we continued our studies, perhaps moving to a different university, and embarked on a long period of research (a minimum of three years full-time, and in practice often taking longer) leading to a doctorate (DPhil/PhD = doctor of philosophy/philosophiae doctor). Then we applied for posts in universities. There are three-year research fellowships, especially at Oxford and Cambridge, and funded by the British Academy, giving young scholars a further three years to pursue their research and to do a little teaching. Many universities employ temporary fixed-term or part-time teachers and such employment may give you a start. But what you hope for is a full-time permanent university lectureship. Vacancies crop up when existing lecturers die, retire or move on; and, more rarely nowadays, when a university decides to increase the numbers of lecturers it has in any subject. Once you are a lecturer, you can hope to be promoted to Senior Lecturer and then to Reader and finally to Professor: appointments to Professor are also made by open competition, so you can apply for a Chair – to be appointed as a Professor – in another university. (Oxford University is different in that all lecturers are also Fellows of a college, and often are described as Fellows rather than as lecturers.) Here I shall use the word 'lecturer' to mean anyone who is employed by a university to teach and to research, including professors (rather than just those lecturers who have not yet been promoted).

So we became university lecturers after doing a period of advanced study – research – and as lecturers we teach our specialist interest and we have time to develop it further. But what does 'research' – this term I have been using freely – mean in practice? It is a somewhat misleading word, more apt in the physical sciences where it can mean carrying out controlled experiments in order to test relationships and hypotheses. In my field, history, what it means is that we are studying intensively, spending a great deal of time reading, thinking, doing things at first hand, not relying on other people's books, but testing, checking, looking for new patterns and connections, appraising, discussing our own hypotheses with other scholars both in our home university and in universities all over the world, and publishing our findings in books and articles; and doing so with energy and passion. We are not just keeping abreast of what is going on in our fields, we are ourselves contributing to those developments.

Let me illustrate from my own experience. My research concentrates on religion and politics in the reign of Henry VIII. For example, I studied the fall of Anne Boleyn, Henry VIII's second queen. In 1536 she was accused of multiple adulteries, including incest with her brother, was convicted and executed. Most historians who have written on the subject have seen Anne as wholly innocent and these charges as the inventions of her enemies who were determined to bring her down. When teaching the period I summarised such interpretations. But I felt uneasy. Why was it so obvious, I mused, that Anne was innocent? And a few years later a colleague drew my attention to an account in verse by a Frenchman in the service of the French ambassador at London at the time of Anne's fall. As he presented it, Anne was indeed guilty of adultery, and her misdemeanours were revealed as a result of a chance quarrel between one of the Queen's ladies and her brother. I then scrutinised other sources very carefully and it seemed to me that a very plausible case could be made in support of Anne's guilt. I wrote an article, published in the *English Historical Review* (1991), offering my reasons.

Let me offer another example. Sir Geoffrey Elton (1921–1994), perhaps the greatest Tudor historian of the twentieth century, saw Thomas

Cromwell, Henry VIII's minister, as a reforming genius who dominated government and politics in the 1530s. I looked carefully at a large number of surviving 'remembrances', notes that Cromwell made of things to be done, and I was struck how often Cromwell noted that he should ask the King's pleasure. That led me to argue that Cromwell, far from ruling in the King's name, on his own initiative, was very much Henry VIII's servant. My arguments were published in *History* (1998).

I have gone on at some length about my own researches in order to illustrate the detail, the depth, and the range of reflection involved in such studies, which I should claim are typical of university teachers. Ask any university teacher about his or her research – 'What are you researching?', or better still, 'What have you had published most recently ?' – and you will get comparable illustrations.

Why and how does the fact that we as teachers are also researchers affect you? Why have I thought it important to dwell on this? The principal reason is that you as students will be the first and direct beneficiaries of our research. I do not simply mean that my students are the first to hear, in a lecture, my latest arguments, though that is obviously true. It is more that the 'research', the systematic and questioning study that I undertake, which leads in time to the publication of books and articles, can also be seen as sustained preparation for teaching. For many years I have been preparing and writing what will be a substantial book on the Henrician Reformation and teaching a third-year Special Subject based on students' close study of printed sources on that topic. Whenever I read and reflect on religion and politics in the reign of Henry VIII and so add to my own learning, what I am doing *at the same time* contributes both to my book and to my teaching. And that congruence of research and teaching is typical of university lecturers in general.

This also matters to you because it affects our expectations of our students. We should like to discuss with our students what we have found in our own studies. We pay you the compliment of treating you like ourselves, or rather as only slightly less experienced scholars than ourselves. That means that you need to have done a fair amount of work to be in a position to grasp and comment. To be able to comment on my articles on Anne Boleyn and Thomas Cromwell, it would be very helpful if you had read a good deal of what has previously been written on those topics. My articles were in many ways a critical commentary on the books and articles of others, especially Eric Ives on Anne Boleyn and Geoffrey Elton on Cromwell, and so you would need to have read them in order fully to appreciate my arguments. And as you can see, historians like myself are involved in dialogue – even argument – with other historians; you need to be able to make sense of the debates.

Obviously at university we do give lectures, including introductory lectures, and there may be more of that in the sciences, but what we do not do is spoon-feed you. We do not say 'Here is a handout that contains all you need to know – just memorise it, and you will pass'. Sadly in many schools what teachers seem to do is to dictate notes, or distribute handouts – summaries on virtually every aspect of the subject that is likely to come up in an examination, tell their pupils to learn them off by heart, and then repeatedly test them. Not surprisingly, most find this very boring. What place is there for finding things out for yourself, what scope is there for grasping that there may be more than one side to a question, or for organising your own studies? Consequently it is a poor preparation for university because it does not prepare you very well for dealing unaided with the kinds of debates between scholars that I have just described.

We obviously expect our students to follow our guidance – but more importantly we expect them to find out the basic information themselves, to find the books and articles they need, and to get on with their reading; in other words to study independently. For example, if you are discussing whether Henry VIII was puppet or puppeteer, whether he was in charge or whether he was being manipulated by political factions, you do need first to know when Henry reigned, the key facts about his reign, his wives, his ministers and courtiers, the main events – but we expect you to know how to find that basic information yourselves. What we want to discuss with you are the more interesting and more complex aspects of the reign, such as the relative merits of different interpretations of the fall of Anne Boleyn, but we cannot do that effectively unless you have laid the groundwork by grasping the basics yourselves. We want you to sort out your own thoughts, and to write essays to cover the syllabus, not without our help, but very much on your own, coming up with your own ideas.

Here at university there is a difference between the science students who tend to have very structured days – mornings in the lecture room, afternoons in the laboratory – and arts and social science students who will rarely have more than say ten hours a week (often fewer) in the class room – some lectures, some seminars/classes/tutorials (I shall explain more precisely what these terms mean later) – and consequently will have a great deal more free time than they are used to at school. But humanities and social science students are very much expected to get on with it. Here, we say, is an essay topic, a list of books and articles:

read as many of them as you can, and submit an essay in a fortnight. Of course some school sixth forms are like that – mine was. I do not remember asking for help on writing essays from my teachers, but if you are used to very detailed assistance when you are preparing an assignment, expect to change your ways at university. What we do rather is to discuss your ideas with you – in classes, in tutorials – and comment critically on them – when we mark, and copiously annotate, your essays.

My experiences as a researching historian affect my approach to teaching in another sense. I am constantly questioning what I think I know, not accepting that just because it says in a book that something is such-and-such that it really is. Instead, I ask how convincing is the assertion? What is the evidence for it? What is the precise wording? Could it be interpreted another way? I try to understand all sides of an argument. In a matter of controversy I pay special attention to those who put forward points opposed to mine, in case they might be right. Where this affects my teaching is that I expect my students to be aware of such debates, not to write essays (for example) that show no awareness that anyone has disagreed with what they are saying; and what counts for me is not whether a student agrees with my ideas but rather the skill with which a student justifies his or her own conclusions – and few things impress me more than a well-reasoned and well-supported essay that disagrees with my own arguments.

My experience as a researching historian makes me ever curious about what other specialists in my field are up to. I regularly go to bookshops, especially in Oxford and London, to browse through recently published books, and I often buy and read them through; similarly I keep up with historical periodicals – articles – in which historians present their findings, and book reviews, both in historical journals, and in the newspapers, and obviously I think about them, discuss them, sometimes write in criticism of them; and again I expect my students to be aware that my subject consists of such continuing publication and debate.

As a university teacher and researching historian I have, I hope, never stopped learning about my subject, and particularly those aspects in which I have specialised, and I hope that I have learned a good deal, which I can share with my students. As Sir Michael Howard (the military historian, formerly Regius Professor of Modern History at Oxford) has pointed out, the true function of universities is not teaching or research as such, but *learning*, 'the accumulation, the sifting and transmission of knowledge'. Here the word 'knowledge' does not simply mean factual knowledge (of the kind tested in a television quiz show). It does include finding out detailed information – and if your aim is not to take things on trust, that is a more challenging aim than you might suppose. Learning also involves reflecting on what is known and what has been learned – seeking patterns, trying to answer difficult questions ('Why has there been such an expansion of the universities since the 1960s?'), reconsidering inherited views. What I seek to do – and what you as a student would be doing – is quite simply learning, getting to grips with what there is to know about the subject you have chosen, thinking about it, and offering my thoughts about it.

So you should think of going on to university if you are committed and enthusiastic about the subject or subjects you wish to study, and if you would like the experience of learning under the guidance of scholars who are learning too (though because of their experience, at a higher level). If when you are set a new essay to prepare, or when you see a book on the subject you are writing, you feel a thrill of excitement and adventure; if when you get down to your studies, you are so absorbed by them that you forget the time, then you are made for studying at university.

Make your choice of subject (or subjects) that you will study *positively*, because you find studying it (or them) rewarding, not because you vaguely think it might be useful in looking for a job later, or because you happen to have got your best marks in school in it.

Do not be put off a subject just because it is not obviously vocational. Of course, some degree subjects, for example, medicine, veterinary science, engineering, are essential if you want to become a doctor, a vet or an engineer, and are rarely taken by anyone who does not wish to pursue such careers. But other vocational degrees, such as law, accountancy, business studies, are far from compulsory even if you want to become a lawyer or an accountant or go into business, and, arguably, you would do better to take a rigorous non-vocational subject (such as history) as your degree course, and then study for your vocational qualifications in law, accountancy or business studies after graduating. And it is worth adding here that vocational degrees do not always guarantee employment in your chosen vocation. Some 12,000 students graduate in law each year; in addition some 2000 graduates take the one-year conversion course for graduates in other subjects. These 14,000 are then eligible to compete for 7000 places on the one-year legal practice courses for would-be solicitors, and the 1500 places on the Bar vocational courses for trainee barristers. Roughly half the would-be solicitors will be able to join solicitors' firms on two-year training contracts, and roughly half the would-be barristers will be able to join barristers' chambers on pupillage (*Times*

Higher, 21 January 2000). But that means that only between a third and a quarter of graduates in law are likely to find employment as solicitors or barristers. If that is what you want to do, because you are excited by the law, then my advice is to go for it (though maybe through the graduate conversion route), without being put off by the odds against; but if you are by no means sure that you want to become a lawyer, do not let yourself be persuaded that a degree in law is a vocational degree that is sure to lead you to a good job, especially if you are not really very interested in law, and if studying it would, for you, be something of a grind.

Studying at university is about studying a demanding subject for its own sake, on its own merits. That, as I have been showing in this chapter, is what characterises the lecturers who will be teaching you. Studying at university is not something that should be undertaken tactically, because of something else, as a sort of unpleasant but ultimately beneficial medicine.

Chapter 3

Why some universities are better than others

How universities are funded

You have decided to go to university. But which one? There are so many and it seems very difficult to decide between them. This chapter is intended to offer some advice. It will do so indirectly. I shall begin by describing the ways in which universities are funded, because funding, I shall argue, should play a crucial part in your decision.

What funds do universities need? To begin with they needed enough to pay the lecturers, to maintain the buildings needed for teaching, and, later, to develop libraries. Rents from charitable bequests of land from kings, queens, churchmen, landowners and merchants, together with fees paid by better-off students met these costs. In the nineteenth century many industrialists and businessmen made large gifts. But by the early twentieth century it was clear that such funding was insufficient to pay for increasingly important but expensive scientific and technological research. The state stepped in. In the United Kingdom from 1919 onwards central government has made grants to the universities from the revenues it raises by taxation. So important has state funding become that the universities, while legally independent and autonomous bodies, are now in practice wholly dependent on such funding for their core functions and are in effect departments of state. (Many universities also receive substantial funding for specific research projects, especially in medicine, the sciences and engineering, from non-governmental sources, but few could survive, and in particular offer teaching, on such contract funding alone.)

The procedures by which governments distribute money to the universities are highly complex and are frequently changed. At present the Government allocates a sum annually to the Higher Education Funding Council for England, to the Scottish Higher Education

Funding Council and to the Northern Ireland Office. This sum is then distributed according to assessments of the research done in different universities and according to the numbers of students in each university. Some subjects are cheaper, some more expensive; and each university is told the maximum number of students it can admit in each subject and receive funding for (since the Government is anxious that public expenditure limits are not breached). In addition, what is called a tuition fee, set by the Government, is charged for each student. From 1998–99 students (unless exempted on grounds of low incomes) have been required to pay this tuition fee: the rate was set at £1000 in 1998–99, and has risen to £1100 in 2002–03. Though this payment is called a tuition fee, it amounts to only a quarter of the funds allocated to universities for teaching, and only between ten and 20 per cent of the total funds allocated by the Government to universities once research funding is taken into account. In other words, the tuition fee would have to be between five and ten times higher if universities were to be funded, at current levels of expenditure, wholly by fees paid by students, and even higher if a British university wished to compete with Princeton or Yale. All these financial arrangements are tightly controlled by the Government: universities by law are not allowed to charge higher fees, although there have been occasional hints that the Government might contemplate relaxing such restrictions.

Universities also contract themselves out to perform all manner of research and services. Industrial companies or charitable bodies award grants to universities to carry out research on their behalf, especially in medicine, technology and the sciences: universities may retain a share of the grants as 'overheads' towards their general expenses. Universities use their student accommodation for conferences during the vacations, earning significant income. Universities have thus in a sense become large businesses, receiving and spending large sums of money, and employing large numbers of people.

By and large governments in the last generation – for the last 25 years – have not given universities enough money, so that the quality of university research and teaching has been significantly affected. University teachers' salaries have fallen compared with those of (say) civil servants or journalists or accountants, let alone stockbrokers, lawyers or doctors. Total expenditure on universities has risen, but if that spending is divided by the numbers of students, a different picture emerges: spending per student has fallen relentlessly. There are obvious failings in infrastructure, as a walk round most universities quickly reveals, though the situation is not as bad as in NHS hospitals. The effects of this prolonged financial squeeze have been uneven: different universities have been affected in different ways.

All that may seem interesting but not especially relevant to prospective students. But it is in fact highly important. Where we are now in large part reflects the experiences of the past. What different universities have inherited from the past is highly diverse. Student numbers, and the rate of growth of student numbers, vary considerably. Above all there are considerable, and growing, differences between those universities best and worst funded. It is funding, both current levels of funding, and inherited accumulated funding, more than anything else, that makes one university better than another. That is especially true given that even those universities in receipt of the largest sums of money have over the past generation been receiving less and less in real terms, and, in comparison with the great American universities, are not well-off at all. Instead of writing about 'richer' or 'best funded' universities, it would be more honest to describe them as 'less poor'. When you are choosing a university, look very carefully at its overall funding, along the lines I shall shortly indicate.

Why university league tables are misleading

Ignore those league tables published in the papers which attempt to rank universities by combining a dozen or more so-called performance indicators. They reflect more the efforts of newspapers to inflate their sales than any reliable rankings. Such calculations are often crudely executed and based on questionable criteria. One newspaper uses the percentage of first-class degrees awarded by a university as a performance indicator; another uses the percentage of first- and upper second-class degrees combined. But how useful a guide for you in choosing a university is this? Does it tell you that the best teaching is to be found at the universities with the highest percentage of firsts – or firsts and upper seconds combined – or does it simply reveal that more good students chose those universities? One newspaper uses the ratio of applications to places as a performance indicator. An immediate problem is that Oxford and Cambridge receive fewer applications per place than many other universities: that is because they are thought to be difficult to get into, not because they are not good universities. And the geographical location of universities makes a great difference to the numbers of applications. Another performance indicator used by one newspaper is the proportion of foreign students: it is hard to see the relevance of this. Another criterion used is the percentage of staff who hold permanent contracts: the awkwardness here is that this places universities with large numbers of fixed-term research staff, common in universities in which many scientific, medical and engineering projects are taking place, at the bottom of the ranking. And in order to derive the league tables that make for eye-catching headlines, all these disparate performance indicators have to be lumped together. Canny university administrators are beginning to treat them as a game, trying to manipulate the figures (sometimes in ways that are by no means helpful, for example limiting the scope for admissions tutors to admit students with lower than expected A-level grades in order to raise the average A-level score at entry).

Even the official surveys of research and teaching, organised by the Higher Education Funding Council and equivalent quangos in Scotland, Wales and Northern Ireland, are themselves deeply flawed.

Successive Research Assessment Exercises (RAEs) have ranked university departments by subject, most recently giving the best 5*, the next best 5, and so on all the way down to 1. In the sciences, medicine and engineering, this seems to be thought reasonably fair, though it is sometimes felt that the limited number of grades exaggerates the often very small differences between departments. A department rated 4 might more fairly be rated 4.4 and another rated 5 might more fairly be rated 4.6, I have been told, which, if true, weakens the usefulness of RAE ratings for your purposes. In the humanities and social sciences, they are much more problematic still. When you are choosing which university to apply to, the grade a department received in the last RAE does not tell you anything very reliable about it. The Modern History Faculty at Oxford was graded at 4 in 1992, 5* in 1996, and 5 in 2001: yet it is highly unlikely that the character and quality of the research achieved by its members really varied so greatly over that period, and however fine the research of the 12 members of the history department at Oxford Brookes University, which was graded at 5* in 2001, it is hard to believe that anyone would seriously claim that that department was really superior to the modern history faculty at Oxford.

The difficulty lies in the way these assessments have to be made. Scholars in the humanities, in most of the social sciences, and also beyond, study as individuals, not as members of departmental teams, and their research is necessarily highly specialised: there is consequently an artificiality in publishing a rating that is an overall assessment of a whole department. For example, in order to produce its rankings, the panel assessing history looks at the lists of publications – up to four over the previous six years – of those submitted for the exercise – and grades each individual historian on a points' score from 5 (best) down to 1 (worst): the scores are then aggregated to produce an overall grade for each department. The difficulty the panellists face is that the general level of writing by historians employed in British universities is of a high 'professional' standard. Historians who publish any reasonable research based on study in the sources are hard to deny a grade 4. But grades of 5 – for an especially good piece of work – or grade 3 – for something less substantial or less original – rest on inescapably subjective judgements. Think of books that you and your friends have read: imagine that you were assessing them in this way, and see how far you would be in agreement on your ratings. Yet on such a procedure turns the overall grade given to departments. Do not take them seriously as a guide to where to apply. And be wary of thinking that any department graded 5 must necessarily be a better place to study than one graded 4. Shortly I shall suggest more helpful ways of judging between universities.

But first we must consider another 'performance indicator', the Funding Council's (now the Quality Assurance Agency's) Teaching Quality Assessments (TQAs) which have been even more fraught than the RAEs. In 1993 the Funding Council began a cycle of assessments of teaching in universities, subject by subject: the cycle was completed in 2001. At first, departments' teaching was labelled 'excellent', 'satisfactory' or 'unsatisfactory' overall; more recently departments have got marks out of four under six different headings. When a department's teaching was described as 'excellent' or when it has scored 24 out of 24, then much is made of this in the brochures that you will see. But all this is quite misleading as a guide to prospective students as to where you will find good teaching and good conditions in which to study – and it is effectively being abolished from 2002. Nevertheless the assessments that were carried out over the previous ten years – at the time of writing they may be consulted on the QAA's webpages at http://www.qaa.ac.uk – remain on file: departments and universities will no doubt continue to trumpet their past successes, and these assessments continue to play a significant part in newspaper league tables.

What has been wrong with TQAs? Why should you place no faith in them? Quite simply because it is very hard to measure the quality of teaching, and because, in my view, the way in which TQAs tried to do that did not work.

Remember that these TQA labels or grades were given to whole departments – in my subject typically as many as 20 or 30 history lecturers, and in some universities many more – not to individuals. Yet teaching is done by individuals: a lecturer delivering a lecture or taking a class usually does so as an individual. Remember that the difference between departments rated 'excellent' and those rated 'satisfactory', or those scoring 24 out of 24 and those scoring 18 out of 24 – which is the case for all but an infinitesimal number – is emphatically not between 'good' and 'bad' teaching, but between varying shades of professionally competent teaching. And how reliable are the judgements that say that one department is worth 23 out of 24, another 21 out of 24 and another 18 out of 24? Is there really any great difference?

Who makes these judgements? Panels of assessors were chosen from university teachers, but one could argue that this is a chore that attracts a certain type of individual, someone who likes telling people what to do and often has very definite views of how teaching should be carried out. Groups of four or five assessors spent two or three days in a department. They observed a few lectures and classes – but it is notoriously difficult to evaluate – and certainly to grade – the quality of teaching.

Think of your own teachers. How would you rate them on a points score? How confident would you be in your ratings? Would your classmates all agree with you – or would there be wildly differing estimates? Probably there would be agreement if a teacher was hopelessly bad. A bad teacher is usually one who is not doing what he or she ought to do. A bad teacher comes to classes late, is unprepared, does not know his or her subject, cannot (in a school) maintain order, does not mark homework promptly or carefully, does not seem to care about the pupils and does the least that he or she can get away with. Such incompetent individuals are rare in secondary schools, and rarer still in universities. But where they are found there is, I fear, not much that can be done to improve them: the crucial thing is to take great care whenever vacancies are filled so that no one like that is ever appointed.

What is much more common is that teachers operate at a sound professional level, with varying strengths and weaknesses. Then, for most of us, there are one or two teachers who are something special, who inspire us by what they are, by the force of their personality more than by what they actually say. Here there may well be sharp disagreements between pupils. I became an historian largely because I was taught by an inspiring history teacher at school. By his example, by his obvious enthusiasm for his subject, by talking with energy and sincerity about what interested him, and by his kindness and encouragement to us, he made me think history worth studying. My debt to him is incalculable. But such enthusiastic teaching, a priceless quality, is not something that can be achieved by training courses: all an enlightened government can do is to foster the general conditions in which such enthusiasm can flourish (and in my opinion no government in my working lifetime has done that). There is still a further problem here: not everyone is moved by a teacher in the same way. A very good friend of mine, who also has gone on to become a university lecturer, disliked that teacher, quite irrationally in my view, but nonetheless quite sincerely. Suppose we were teaching assessors – I should have graded my teacher as excellent, but my friend would not. Which of us was right? Teaching necessarily involves a relationship between teacher and pupil, and, like any human relationship, one that is complex and unpredictable.

What is good teaching? Does everyone agree? A small illustration from the TQA visit to my department helps to illustrate the problems. A colleague held a seminar, a double-hour class to which four students presented short papers followed by a general discussion, which my colleague felt went well. The assessor was not so sure. Should you not have divided the class up into four groups, set them each different tasks, let them sort them out amongst themselves, and then report back to the full group? A recent guide to good teaching suggests that all lecturers should break up their lectures – no one can concentrate for an hour, it asserts – divide the audience into small groups, and set each 'buzz-group' a series of small tasks to perform. I personally find such suggestions inappropriate. When I went to a lecture as a student, and when I go to a lecture or a seminar or conference paper now, I expect a full-length address from the speaker. I am interested in what the speaker has to say about his or her subject, and I am quite prepared to concentrate. If I want to follow something up, I am more than ready to do so in the library later. But I do not want to waste time doing it rather inefficiently, cut off from access to books, while in a lecture room. But which style do you prefer? Which do you think makes for better teaching?

Since making judgements on individuals' teaching is so tricky, TQAs have tended to concentrate on procedures and on paperwork. Are there clear descriptions of the 'aims' and 'objectives' of each course taught in a department? What precise skills does each course seek to convey? Are the 'intended learning outcomes' of each class ('what students can be expected to know or do at the end that they did not know or could not do at the beginning') clearly and exactly set out in relation to 'a structured programme of content and learning activities' so that the results of their learning and the teaching they have received can be clearly demonstrated and measured? How effectively is the curriculum 'delivered'?

In my view all that reflects a damagingly skewed and philistine view of the nature of university education. To reduce every class to a set of 'learning outcomes' is to turn a complex process into a miscellany of trivial bits, and to overlook the importance of making connections. It risks limiting what is studied to what can be assessed and what can be measured: that is the approach of the accountant who knows the price of everything and the value of nothing. To speak of 'curriculum delivery' is to make a misplaced analogy with mail-order van drivers delivering goods that have been ordered by phone or e-mail. But learning requires substantial mental activity on the part of the learner, not just a simple act of ordering and then of opening the door to receive a pre-packaged parcel of knowledge. Successful 'learning outcomes' depend on students studying and learning and thinking for themselves. And there is only so much that their teachers can do: you can lead a horse to water but you cannot make it drink. Not only are such criteria flawed, but, worse still, departments are judged on how closely they conform to such mistaken criteria. If they dissent – if they believe that teaching is an art, not the application of a methodology, if they believe that the ultimate aim of all university education is to foster a critical intelligence – that is held against them. If they protest that cuts in government funding are making it impossible to teach to the standards they used to maintain, for example compelling them to reduce the number of classes students are offered, then they risk being told, as one department was, that 'staff–student contact time is, by national standards, still somewhat generous'.

All this encourages universities to lie and to cheat, as Noel Annan has observed, presenting themselves in the best possible light, spinning frantically, and putting on a show for the Government Inspectors. In the early days, it was not uncommon for departments which claimed to be excellent to be rated simply as satisfactory, not least because they were too honest. But more recently, almost all departments have scored highly. Maybe things have improved, or, much more likely, universities have become more skilful in showing themselves and, especially, preparing mountains of paperwork, in ways that conform to the expectations of the inspectors. Do not be fooled.

You would thus be well advised not to take the Funding Council's Teaching Quality Assessment ratings into account when choosing which universities you apply to. By all means read the full reports – though you will have plenty to work through if you do – but read them critically. And do not think that they are 'gospel'. A more technical point is that a great many of them are now out of date. For example departments of history in English universities were assessed as long ago as 1993: the grades reflect assessments made of the staff and syllabuses of 1993, not the present. Since then there will certainly have been high levels of staff turnover and frequent changes in syllabuses. So if you visit a university to which you are thinking of going, ask how much has changed since the last TQA report: any TQA older than, say, five years is unlikely to be very useful.

The funding of research: the best guide

How then should you decide between universities? They are plainly not all the same. Their brochures and webpages make all kinds of increasingly boastful claims. Official assessments of research and teaching are, as I have argued, of doubtful value. Newspapers offer league tables of doubtful validity. There is much folklore and anecdote. Is there any reliable and straightforward way of finding out which universities are the best?

I should claim that there is. What you should take into account above all is research, which, as I suggested in Chapter 2, is the feature that distinguishes universities from schools. But instead of using the flawed Research Assessment Exercises and applying to the University of X because the subject you wish to study has been graded 5 there rather than to the University of Z because there it has been graded 4, look instead at how much money a university receives overall for research from the Funding Councils. Of course, that overall funding does reflect the outcomes of the Research Assessment Exercises in each of the subjects at that university: flawed though they are, the RAEs do unfortunately have important consequences. My claim is quite simply that *the best universities are those that receive the largest sums for research:* what is important for you is to go to the best-funded university that you can. I shall explain why. But first, here is the list of the universities which are receiving the largest sums for research from the Funding Councils: my table shows the grants made in 1997–98, followed by those in 2000–01, 2001–02 and 2002–03. There is – astonishingly – little change, year by year, in the rankings. The top four universities have been given substantially greater research funding – especially University College London and Imperial College London – but most of the others (King's College London is the biggest exception, and no doubt there is some technical explanation for the low figure for 1997–98) have received only small increases, barely matching general inflation. And the pecking order hardly changes.

Table 3.1 Research funding from the Funding Councils (in millions of pounds)

	1997–98	2000–1	2001–2	2002–03
Oxford	53	64	65	65
Cambridge	49	63	64	68
University College London	41	63	64	67
Imperial College London	38	55	56	61
King's College London	(18)	37	38	38
Edinburgh	31	n/a	36	38
Manchester	27	32	33	39
Leeds	24	28	28	31
Birmingham	23	27	29	29
Sheffield	22	25	27	30
Bristol	20	24	25	29
Southampton	20	24	25	31
Nottingham	19	23	25	25
Glasgow	20	n/a	23	27
Newcastle	18	21	22	23
Liverpool	16	20	20	22
Cardiff	16	18	19	27
Warwick	15	17	18	20
Strathclyde	13	n/a	14	14
Reading	12	14	14	16
Queen Mary/Westfield London	11	14	14	13
Umist	11	13	13	13
Leicester	10	13	13	13
Durham	10	12	13	16
Sussex	11	12	12	12
Queen's Belfast	11	n/a	n/a	n/a
York	10	12	12	15
Bath	10	11	11	12
Lancaster	10	11	11	12
Surrey	8	11	11	14

Adapted from material in *Times Higher*, 3 December 1999, 3 March 2000, 2 March 2001, 8 March 2002, 22 March 2002, 29 March 2002. Rank order is that for 2000–01: table lists universities receiving £11 million or more that year.

In 2002–03, Dundee's allocation is £12 million (£9 million in 1997–98), London School of Economics £12 million (£8 million in 1997–98), East Anglia and Loughborough £11 million (both £8 million in 1997–98). The new university receiving the largest grant in 1997–98, Portsmouth, received only £2.6 million that year, £2.8 million in 2000–01, and £3.7 million for 2001–02, in which year it is just overtaken by Greenwich, also receiving £3.7 million; Wolverhampton (where I once taught) received only £213,000 in 1997–98, £354,000 in 2000–01 and £337,000 for 2001–02.

To assess those figures fairly it would of course be necessary to know how many staff and how many students there were at each university. They are not all the same size. Some universities are small or restrict themselves to a small number of subjects, so they will not show up highly in a table listing total funding, which will obviously favour universities with faculties of medicine and engineering. The London School of Economics, for example, received £12 million in 2002–03, but since it concentrates on the social sciences, that is a high sum for what it does.

So another way of listing the best funded universities is to look at what percentage of their total income from the Funding Councils is given for research (see Table 3.2 on page 32).

The London School of Economics comes out well here. Cranfield and Surrey are specialist universities; East Anglia and Essex are relatively small.

These rankings offer you valuable guidance. But remember that universities close to one another in the scale are much the same: Oxford received a little more than Cambridge, both in cash and as a percentage, but the proper deduction to make from these rankings is that Oxford and Cambridge are pretty much equals in terms of funding, rather than any crude newspaper headline of the sort 'Oxford beats Cambridge in photo finish'. And all the universities whose percentage is, say, in the low thirties, or in the mid-twenties, are on this measure much the same. Newspapers love headlining changes – 'Barsetshire leaps ten places this year' – but such headlines are not helpful indicators for you.

Why research funding matters for students

Why are these rankings by far the most useful to consider for you as a prospective applicant? Why should the funding of universities for research, and the proportion of their funding that comes for research, be so revealing an indicator? You may at first suppose that since what most interests you as a student is the teaching you will get, the fact that one

Table 3.2 Percentage of total income from Funding Councils

	1997–98	2002–03
Oxford	60	54
Cambridge	56	54
University College London	48	54
London School of Economics	46	60
Imperial College London	42	55
Umist	40	39
York	38	43
Bristol	36	37
Sheffield	36	37
Warwick	36	40
Edinburgh	36	34
Bath	34	33
King's College London	34	39
Lancaster	34	34
Nottingham	34	32
Sussex	34	34
Birmingham	32	33
Essex	32	32
Leeds	32	30
Reading	32	40
Southampton	32	41
Surrey	32	43
Cranfield	30	25
East Anglia	30	36
Manchester	30	39
Newcastle	30	33
Cardiff	30	37
Durham	28	31
Leicester	28	31
St Andrews	28	36
Dundee	26	25
Keele	26	26
Liverpool	26	29
Royal Holloway	26	38
Glasgow	24	26
Loughborough	24	25
Queen Mary/Westfield London	24	24
Swansea	24	27

Adapted from material in *Times Higher* (3 December 1999); second column author's calculations from figures in *Times Higher* (8 March 2002, 22 March 2002, 29 March 2002).

university receives more funding than another for research does not have much do with you. But it does.

Universities receive the same amount for teaching a student in any given subject. There are just two qualifications to this. First, Oxford and Cambridge colleges have long received an additional college fee for every student: this is being phased out and replaced by a larger general grant to both universities. Secondly, since 2002, universities have been paid a higher amount – currently 5 per cent more – for each student they recruit from a socially disadvantaged area, defined by those (unpublished) postcode areas from which currently the smallest percentage of students come. But, apart from these variations, every university that admits students to study history will receive the same amount for each student from the Funding Council for teaching them. But that does not mean that wherever students study history, roughly the same amount of public money will be spent in supporting their studies. That is because funding for research, unlike that for teaching, is, as we have seen, quite deliberately unequal. So while all universities receive the same for teaching in a subject, they receive very different amounts for research in that subject. Of course, research funding is intended for research. But teaching and research are far too closely interrelated for so rigid a separation to be possible in practice.

It is manifestly the case that those universities that get the most funds for research will be the universities with the most money overall to spend. The research funding universities receive from the Funding Council comes as a lump sum, with few specific conditions on how it is to be spent. That is left to each university to determine: it can distribute the money exactly according to the gradings given in the Research Assessment Exercises, or it can redistribute, in order to build up weaker departments, the extra funds that a high-rated department has earned. The grade that any individual department has received in the RAE is much less important than the overall level of research funding allocated to the university as a whole. Those universities that overall receive the greatest research funding will be able to spend more on laboratories, equipment, computers and libraries, and above all they will be able to spend more on staff; that is to say that they will be able to employ more lecturers. That will mean that the ratio of staff to students will be more favourable – or, perhaps, less unfavourable – than in universities whose income is lower. Universities with higher levels of research funding are therefore able to offer better teaching than those with lower levels of research funding.

Let me compare my own university, Southampton, with the University of Northumbria at Newcastle, where I recently completed a four-year stint as an external examiner, and take figures from my last year serving there, 2000–01. In that year the number of students funded by the Funding Council was roughly the same at both universities: 12,167 at Southampton and 12,582 at Northumbria. The money these two universities received for teaching was also roughly the same: £38.2 million at Southampton, £37.5 million at Northumbria. Both universities also received much the same in tuition fees: £10.7 million at Southampton, £11.4 million at Northumbria. But there was a huge difference in the funds that the two universities received for research. Southampton received £24 million; Northumbria received £1.5 million. That shows that the total income each university receives from the Funding Council and from fees is very different. In my example, Southampton received £73 million, Northumbria received £50 million. If you go on to divide the total sums received by each university by the number of students, on that calculation, Southampton had nearly £6000 per student, Northumbria £4000 per student. The explanation for the difference lies in the funding the two universities receive for research. (In passing, note that Oxford and Cambridge in 2000–01 received roughly £12,500 per student.) Such calculations offer a very revealing impression of the general conditions that students can expect to find in different universities.

Let me offer a simplified illustration of what differential funding for research means in practice. Suppose both the University of Barsetshire (set in the county town of the leafy county of Barsetshire) and Coketown New University (in what was once a mining region) admit 100 students each year to study English literature. Both universities will receive the Funding Council's standard payment for a student studying English multiplied by a hundred, together with the tuition fee for each student. Maybe Coketown will get a little more since many of its students come from disadvantaged areas and so bring with them the 5 per cent postcode premium. Now look at the funding for research. Coketown New University typically receives a tiny amount – perhaps nothing at all. The University of Barsetshire, however, receives a good deal of money for research. Universities are given these funds as a lump sum, and they are free within limits to spend it as they wish (though if they are funded to admit 100 students, they must honour that obligation). Both universities will employ lecturers to teach their 100 students English literature. But since Barsetshire has more money to spend, it will be able to employ more lecturers than Coketown.

That will mean, first, that those lecturers at Barsetshire will not need to teach as many hours each as their counterparts at Coketown, simply because there are more of them. They will also be able to concentrate their teaching in their specialist interests, rather than having to spread their energies too thinly across a diverse and unconnected range of courses. They will have relatively more time to devote to preparation and to their own learning – or research – and they will have more time to turn their researches into publications, which will in turn mean that the next time that a Research Assessment Exercise measures the research achieved in the universities, the Department of English Literature at Barsetshire will outshine the English Studies Subject Division at Coketown, and so receive greater funding for the future. From a student's point of view, all that means is that if you are at Barsetshire your teachers are more likely to be at the cutting edge of their subject, and you are more likely to benefit from that in their lectures and classes, than if you were at Coketown. On the other hand, the picture might not be quite as rosy as this sketch suggests, because although better funded than Coketown, Barsetshire has also suffered substantial cuts in funding, and its dependence on research funding means that its lecturers are under great pressure to publish in order to maintain it.

Secondly, the greater funding means that the ratio of staff to students will be more favourable at Barsetshire than at Coketown. 'Less unfavourable' would be a more honest description, since Barsetshire has been compelled (as governments have year by year reduced what it pays a university to teach a student) to take in more and more students to maintain its income, while reducing the number of lecturers to cut its costs. Consequently staff:student ratios have significantly worsened at Barsetshire: they are now comparable to what they were at Coketown ten to fifteen years ago. But at Coketown the financial pressures have been even greater and conditions even less favourable. What that means is that if you go to Coketown you are likely to be taught in even larger classes than at Barsetshire.

Of course, small classes are not always better than large classes, but usually they are. Students lacking in confidence will be less likely to take part the larger the group; work-shy students will find it easier to do little. Your teachers will be under too much pressure to give you personal and individual guidance as a matter of course. You will be set less work in a poorer university – you might not see that as a disadvantage of course – because the teachers just could not cope with the volume of marking if more assignments were set. You are more likely to experience what is called 'student-centred learning' or 'open and flexible learning', meaning that you will be left to get on with it with relatively little personal contact from your lecturers, but given 'learning resource materials', i.e. exercises (printed, videos, tapes, inter-active computer-based, CD-ROMS, on the Internet) to work through, without set deadlines, and to 'self-assessment', meaning that no one will read and mark the work you do, but that you will yourself mark it against a set of answers. All this may conceivably have some advantages for particular students – perhaps especially any who because of their personal circumstances can neither devote themselves full-time to study nor attend regularly – but essentially they are being promoted because they are apparently much cheaper for universities to operate than methods which rely on students having regular contact with lecturers and access to libraries full of books. It may have some point in technical subjects in which there is a straightforward body of knowledge to be learned, or worked through mechanically. But even on its own terms, 'open learning' is problematic, since the construction of 'learning resource materials' is far more time-consuming and challenging than one might suppose. After all, it demands that a teacher prepares something like a major textbook. If the 'learning resource materials' you are given are poorly thought through, then the rationale is undermined. Moreover, if what you want to do is to get thoroughly to grips with a traditional subject such as history or literature or physics, then no amount of 'learning resource materials' packaged up for you is going to give you what your own reading of books and articles in a well-stocked library can provide.

Also, the staff in a less well-funded university may well feel demoralised and bitter because of never-ending financial crises and institutional reorganisations, and, even if they do not take out their discontents on you, they will no doubt offer less than they might in happier circumstances. More of the teaching staff will be on fixed-term or part-time contracts. Poorer universities tend to be more chaotically organised because staff and facilities are stretched to breaking point (in one notorious case a university apparently failed even to keep proper records of how many students it had or what courses they were taking: *Daily Mail*, 13 November 1999). A poorer university will have worse libraries and laboratories than a less poor university. Every so often, the Government, in a fit of conscience, and prodded by the poorer universities, makes some slight attempt at redistribution in their favour, but this is no more than sticking plaster over a thousand cuts. Beware those newspaper headlines such as 'New universities start to overthrow the old order' and articles claiming that the top new universities have 'come of age': what that turns out to mean is that in the newspaper's league table two or three new universities have come out slightly higher than two or three of the old universities (e.g. *FT*, 8 April 2000). A glance at the funding that they receive for research quickly gives a rather different impression. With a little spin-doctoring, any university can claim to be at or near the top of some performance criterion or other. So it really is important for you to concentrate on getting into the better-funded universities if you can. Not least it matters to you because how well you will be taught and how well you will be looked after will, to a considerable extent, depend on the morale of those who teach you. You can readily see the problems. Lecturers are under increasing pressure to publish research. They have to teach more and more students in larger and larger classes. They have been distracted by Research Assessment Exercises and teaching assessments. And too much of their time and mental energies are spent in committee meetings fighting over university, faculty and departmental policy to deal with financial cuts. What you deserve is enthusiastic lecturers devoted to their studies and their students: you are most likely to find them in those universities less immediately troubled by financial concerns.

How important it is to go to one of the better-off universities depends to some extent on the subject you wish to study. If you study history, you will find the best historians in the country employed teaching history in the universities – perhaps a score have brain-drained abroad, mainly to the US, but there has been a two-way traffic. There are good and active historians in all of Britain's universities, including those less highly rated universities. That is for the simple, if perhaps depressing, reason that there is not much alternative for historians. I cannot easily earn my living as an historian elsewhere: there are very few alternatives. If I became a schoolteacher, I should lose what opportunities I have to pursue research. Only a handful of historians can live by their pen or by the media. Of course, would-be university lecturers in history would ideally prefer to find jobs in the best-funded universities – those in my list above. But vacancies are rare, usually only arising when someone retires, dies or leaves. So lecturers apply wherever vacancies occur, and that may well mean that a very good historian ends up employed in a poorly funded university. Movement is difficult, so most tend to remain in the university in which they got their first job. All that means that the quality of lecturers in history generally is likely to be pretty high. It may well be that the ambitious and dynamic young lecturer whose lot has fallen in a poorly funded university turns over time into a bitter, cynical, demoralised, impoverished (at least in comparison with friends in other professions), frustrated and over-worked has-been, but even such a lecturer is likely to be buoyed up, at least temporarily, if able and committed students come his or her way.

If you take subjects such as economics, or law, or computer science or accountancy, however, it is immediately clear that the best economists or lawyers or computer scientists or accountants are not necessarily to be found in the universities. University lecturers' salaries are so low – the starting salary for lecturers in their mid-twenties in the year 2001–02 was £20,470, the professorial salary range begins around £42,500 – that any good economist could find a job in the City, in a bank, in an industrial firm, in an international organisation, that paid much more, not least with the possibility of bonuses and share options, that any half-decent lawyer could earn double that as a country solicitor, and anyone with an aptitude for computers could do very well as a consultant. Consequently the quality of economics and law and computer science teachers at university is bound to be much more uneven. There will always be individuals so committed to their studies (and possibly with private means) who will shun the wider world, and there will be more who will divide their career between universities and the City and the Bar, but such individuals will in these subjects gravitate to the best-funded universities much more than historians will. So if you want to study economics or law or accountancy or computer science it is more important to go to the best-funded universities than it is for some other subjects. Even so it is in such subject areas, where it is possible for academics to increase their income by accepting lucrative outside consultancies, that there are the greatest risks that academics will skimp their teaching (for example, by not being around, cancelling classes at short notice, not marking students' work quickly) because they are busy with other tasks for which they are being paid by demanding outside employers. That is much less likely in subjects such as history or literature, where the external temptations are far smaller.

Chapter 4

Choosing your university

It matters very much which university you choose. They are not all the same, despite all being called universities. By all means look carefully at the particular subject department in which you wish to study (especially to check that there are not some special features of the syllabus or the types of assessment or some other particular drawback that might bother you). But do not take the league-table placings or the RAE grades or the TQA scores of an individual department too seriously. What matters more (as we have seen in Chapter 3) is how relatively well-funded the university is. My general advice is to go to the best-funded university that you can (given the A-level grades you are likely to get): my broad claim is that the higher the university's overall level of funding, the richer your experience of university life is likely to be.

The two best-funded universities are Oxford and Cambridge and they require further attention. Both have stood to a large extent apart from the recent trends that have been so remorselessly damaging elsewhere. Their funding has been reduced in real terms, but not by as much. Oxford and Cambridge colleges have a long history and over the centuries most of them have received bequests, initially of land, and some of them – notably Trinity College, Cambridge, St John's College, Oxford – are very wealthy corporations indeed. Their income, a share of which is redistributed to poorer colleges, means that total spending on teaching and research is much higher in Oxford and Cambridge than just the sums provided by the Government through the Funding Council. Such inherited wealth has enabled Oxford and Cambridge to withstand the most abrupt cuts in funding that characterised the 1980s. Consequently they resisted the pressure to increase student numbers (it would have been physically difficult in both cities) and staff:student ratios have remained favourable. Moreover, in addition to the usual funding for the teaching of students, Oxford and Cambridge have received college fees (recently turned into a grant to the university centrally that is to be phased out over ten years). Since Oxford and Cambridge have been so much better funded relative to other universities (even if Harvard, Princeton and Yale in America are now vastly wealthier), it is not surprising that Oxford and Cambridge have done best in successive Research Assessment Exercises and so continued to receive the largest allocations of funds for research. Only University College London and Imperial College match them in money, and only the London School of Economics matches them in the percentage of Funding Council income given for research.

For a student, all that means is that the education you are likely to get there is better than you can expect anywhere else. Because they are better off than other universities, they can offer more. At Oxford and Cambridge you are likely to be taught week by week in tutorials either by yourself or with one other student: in other universities you will be lucky indeed if you have classes in single figures. If you are a committed and hard-working student, the opportunities are obvious. Of course, it does not always work: tutorials of this kind are to a greater degree than other forms of teaching a relationship, and if you do not get on with your tutor, it could be a disaster. But the chances are that over three years you will experience the tremendous benefits at some point. It is a very intense form of teaching, much more so than the teaching in less well-funded universities where you meet your lecturers less often, in larger groups and without being expected to come to classes with work prepared anything like as often. Of course, if you are less committed to your studies, you might well be happier elsewhere.

Another feature that makes some uncomfortable is that there are many independent-school educated students at Oxford and Cambridge, and there is obviously still a *Brideshead Revisited* image about Oxbridge. If that bothers you, again you might feel more at ease elsewhere, though my advice would be not to worry about social niceties, but rather to make the most of your studies and opportunities. The high proportion of independent-school educated students at Oxbridge does not reflect prejudice on the part of tutors (there are similarly high percentages of independent-school educated students at other universities, for example Bristol and Durham), but simply that as many as 43 per cent of those getting three As at A level have been to independent schools, even though only 7 per cent of the population is educated in them, and that many of the state-school educated students who achieve the highest A-level grades choose not to apply to Oxbridge. It is just possible that you might encounter – or feel as if you are encountering – some prejudice if you come from a working-class comprehensive school, but it is becoming less and less likely. Most Oxbridge tutors are far from upper-class themselves, and if anything, many of them would now be more sympathetic to promising applicants from state schools and less sympathetic to candidates from independent schools who seem not to have made the most of their undoubted advantages. (Compared with state schools, independent schools have more to spend per pupil, greater freedom to pay staff higher salaries and to dismiss those not pulling their weight, and better facilities: admissions tutors try hard to compensate for this.)

Why is so much fuss made about Oxbridge entrance? Why does it matter when an applicant is rejected? The simple answer is that the experience of being a university student at Oxford and Cambridge is qualitatively different from being a student elsewhere. You may think it odd that in this country we should have just two universities which have accumulated wealth and receive larger grants than the rest: you might think that when the state took on the funding of universities after the First World War, it would have aimed to make each of the newer 'redbrick' universities the equivalent of Oxford and of Cambridge in funding (and not by squeezing Oxford and Cambridge, but by allocating Manchester and Birmingham and Durham and the others funds to allow them to match Oxford and Cambridge, not least bearing in mind their historic endowments). Again you might have thought that when the expansion of the 1960s took place, with new universities such as Sussex and Warwick and York and Lancaster, that successive governments would have funded each new university at the levels of Oxford and Cambridge. But the thrust of government policy has not been to draw on the growing prosperity of the country in order to move on from having two wealthy universities to having first ten, and then 20, and then 30 comparably wealthy universities. Instead governments have again and again created and encouraged the evolution of a hierarchy of a great many universities, with each successive group of new creations being poorer and less well-funded than the previous group. And funding cuts in the past generation together with the vast expansion in student numbers outside Oxford and Cambridge have increased the gap between Oxbridge and the rest. That means that when you are considering applying to university, you must be aware that there are two universities which are and have always been better funded than the rest and are distinctive in character. It would be much better if I could have written here that there were a dozen or two dozen such universities – but the financial figures speak for themselves.

If Oxford and Cambridge put you off, or if you are not quite going to make the high A-level grades they demand, then concentrate on those universities listed in my tables above. Oxbridge apart, they will offer you the best of what is available in British universities. University College London, the London School of Economics, Imperial College, and King's College London are, after Oxbridge, the next best-funded universities. There are then, as my tables above show, some 20 or 30 universities that receive significant levels of research funding. Not surprisingly, the A-level grades that these universities demand are mostly As and Bs. And to be fair, if they cannot match Oxbridge, they can often offer experiences that are very worthwhile, even, in parts, superior to Oxbridge: for example, the third-year special subjects we teach in the Department of History at Southampton, based on intensive study of printed sources, work better, in my opinion, than their Oxford equivalents because they are taken over two terms, not one.

But what if you are not likely to achieve As and Bs and are consequently unlikely to make it into one of the better-funded universities? If you are a committed student, and if your lower A-level grades failed to reflect your true ability and potential, then you can always retake your A levels and try again. That is less common than it was, not least since the more demanding universities have more than enough good first-time applicants to choose from, and since it means spending another year at school, at college or at a crammer. More commonly nowadays, those with disappointing A-level grades are willing to go to almost any university, however poorly funded, and to make the most of it. If you are conspicuously determined and hard-working, your tutors there will almost certainly give you special attention and encouragement. If you are studying a subject such as history or literature, in which the alternatives to university teaching as a career are limited, then (as I have already pointed out) you will almost certainly encounter even at the least well-funded universities lecturers who are as good scholars as you would find in the better-funded universities.

Making your application

What will determine which university you will be able to go to, once you have made your choice, will be your A-level grades, or more immediately, the predictions that your school/college reference writers make about the A-level grades you will secure. You may think that it would be more rational if university entrance were determined *after* you know your A-level results rather than in advance, especially given that references written in October can sum up only one year's study in the sixth form or at college, but all attempts at reform have foundered on the practicalities of getting A-level examinations marked more quickly and university applications processed and accommodation arranged in the time that would be available in the summer. So make your application in consultation with your teachers and in the light of the known marks you have already achieved. There are guides setting out the standard A-level grades sought by each university department: be realistic in framing your own application.

Beyond that there is not a great deal that you can do. Much folklore surrounds the business of applying to university. Ignore most of it. Decisions are made by university lecturers who scrutinise every application. They have quotas to fill but not to exceed: most of the better-funded universities receive far more applications than they have places. So the predicted A-level grades are overwhelmingly the most important factor. Good GCSE results can impress, though selectors may think that the much higher intellectual demands of university study make GCSEs less useful indicators at that level. Performance in the new AS levels is also significant. A strong or a weak reference can on the margin make a difference, but not that much. The reference might perhaps hint that you may yet do better, or it might raise doubts that your good predicted grades reflect the school's cramming rather than your own endeavours. So not every candidate predicted to achieve the department's standard grades will be accepted, nor will every candidate predicted to fall short of them be rejected. It is not true that the *only* thing that admissions selectors look at is the predicted A-level grades. But when all such qualifications have been made, it is also true to say that in most cases the predictions will be the single most important criterion. There is a strong correlation between A-level grades and success at university. It is not a total correlation; you may get three As at A level but get a II:ii or get three Cs but go on to get a first, but surveys consistently show that the most successful university students did well at A level and the least successful university students did not. Only one per cent of students who get three As drop out; some 13 per cent of those who get the equivalent of three Ds do. No wonder, then, that selectors take A-level predictions seriously.

And your personal statement, however much you agonise over it, is not going to make up for predictions of poor A-level grades; in turn it would have to be very weak to pull down good predicted grades. In preparing your self-presentation, imagine that your application is being read by a lecturer committed to research in the way I described in

Chapter 2. What such a scholar will be most impressed by is your own interest in the subject(s) you wish to study. Do not just say that you like literature because you enjoy reading, including Shakespeare and thrillers. Do not just say that you have always liked history and that you enjoy reading and that you liked a recent television history programme. Demonstrate the scope of your reading and your engagement with it:

> My interest in history has been deepened by my project on the Third Reich which has required me to compare the different approaches of biographers of Hitler, notably Bullock, Fest and Kershaw. It has been stimulating trying to determine the relative weight to be given to the actions of an individual and larger social and economic forces.

That shows that you have been reading widely and thinking in general ways about what you have been reading. And remember that it is your intellectual commitment and interests that will most impress university lecturers: do not give a detailed list of all your social and sporting activities or part-time jobs in supermarkets.

Only a few universities, especially Oxford and Cambridge, still use interviews as a general procedure, but if you are invited for an interview, the same points hold there too. Be prepared to talk about the work you have been doing in the subject you wish to study. Be ready, for example, to summarise essays you have recently written, and to talk more generally about the characteristics of the subject. Prepare by imagining that you are the interviewer: what questions would you ask a candidate applying to study the subject you have chosen? Be ready to say why you find a subject interesting and enjoyable. Give the impression that you have found what you have done so far rewarding but that you are very conscious that you have only begun to scratch the surface of the subject and that you would want the chance to do much more. Remember, once again, that you will be interviewed by lecturers who are committed to research and who will be delighted if you show an informed and enthusiastic curiosity in the subject. Practise an interview with your teachers or parents or with your friends: you may feel shy and giggly, but persevere until you relax. If you are going to devote three years of your life to studying a subject at university, you ought to be able to talk fluently and confidently about what you are going to do. It is, it must be recognised, a fact that students from independent schools are often more articulate than those from comprehensive schools, which obviously gives them a competitive advantage in interviews and consequently in the Oxbridge admissions procedure. If you come from a comprehensive school, do not be put off, especially should you on the day meet some brashly self-confident rivals: remember that the admissions tutors are well aware of all this and will rather be trying to compensate for any shyness and hesitancy on your part, especially if you seem eager to learn. But the more you practise beforehand, the more you will build up your confidence.

From time to time politicians and commentators interfere in these procedures. A minister castigates an Oxbridge college for turning down a comprehensive school applicant. A newspaper counters by claiming that Oxbridge college dons discriminate against candidates from independent schools. Another minister hints that universities who recruit predominantly from independent schools will be penalised and the postcode premium greatly increased. Estelle Morris, when Education and Skills Secretary, said that universities should admit comprehensive-school pupils with lower expected A-level grades than those from independent schools. The Department of History at Bristol is reported to be comparing predicted A-level grades with the past average of the school. A climate is developing in which it looks good to be recruiting more state-school pupils. And yet there are conflicting pressures. Governments may speak for state-school applicants, and shift funding at the margin; but university vice-chancellors are increasingly conscious of newspaper league tables which use as a performance indicator the average A-level scores of entrants. If selectors let in too many applicants with poor A levels, the university's place in the league table may be compromised. So there is not a lot you can do. Switching schools just to get an advantage is not to be recommended: it is always disruptive. And there is nothing automatic or certain here. University selectors have always tried to make allowances for applicants with lower predicted grades from difficult backgrounds: if that is your situation, do not hesitate to explain in your personal statement or in a covering letter. If you are an independent-school applicant, try to show that your good predicted A-level grades are not simply the effect of spoon-feeding and drilling by your teachers but reflect your own ability, enthusiasm and determination.

Mature students

Much of what has been suggested so far assumes that you are at school and preparing to apply for university. Yet what if you are not in a position to move around the country, but restricted by personal circumstances to your local university? What if you are not an 18-year-old coming straight from sixth form, but a 'mature student', to use the jargon? Did you, for a variety of reasons, leave school at 16 or 18 and then go straight into employment? But have you since then, not least because you have come to know many past and present students who obviously found studying rewarding, been prompted to ask yourself whether you too would not find further study worthwhile? Are you wondering whether university is for you? And if it is, how should you choose? In particular, is your local – and possibly less well-funded – university worth considering?

If you are thinking of becoming a mature student, seek as much advice as you can. If you have already been working in the areas of employment that graduates traditionally work in – accountancy, management, civil service, local government – but you do not have a degree, then you may well be quite adequately prepared for study at university by the work you have been doing. If you left school young, and if what you have done has not really engaged your mental faculties (be honest and realistic), then you would be wise to test the water first. Your local college will offer all sorts of courses and classes: get a brochure, and ask if you could discuss your options. Enrol for a class. Think of taking A-level courses in the subject or subjects you would be interested in studying at university: that is the best preparation, and also the best indicator to you of what you would be capable of achieving. Many colleges run 'access to higher education' courses, intended to prepare mature students for university entrance: these tend to offer a taste of several different subjects, rather than going into the depth of an A level. Your access tutors will be able to give you advice on what it would be reasonable for you to go on to attempt – though it is as well to remember that they can sometimes be too kind to give you a realistic assessment of your potential.

It is entirely feasible for mature students to go on to Oxford and Cambridge and to the better-funded universities which mainly recruit from 18-year-olds with good A-level grades. In the humanities departments of such universities as many as 10–20 per cent of students are mature students. One possible drawback is that formal examinations are a significant part of assessment: if you have not taken any examinations for years, you may find them quite a strain. Far more mature students go on to local less well-funded universities, often studying part-time, and taking courses largely or wholly assessed by course work (and not examinations). You should still find such study worthwhile.

But some warning is timely. Much depends on the general standards of the students admitted. Since mature students are not recruited by

A-level scores but more commonly on an assessment of their potential on the basis of 'access' courses, there is a risk that some mature students are admitted to degree programmes who are full of enthusiasm but who are not ready for, or perhaps simply not up to, the rigours of university study. (To be fair to mature students, it should be said that some eighteen-year-olds 'peak' at A level, and then show that they too are not ready for, or not up to, a university course.) Less well-funded institutions possess a natural and strong urge for self-preservation: such is their financial plight that they will not turn away students, however unqualified, if they have not filled their quotas. It is not surprising that it is at the least well-funded universities that some scandals have been uncovered (though the number is small and scandals are not in any sense typical). For lecturers, it can be heartbreaking to see enthusiastic mature students whose commitment is not matched by their ability. And if those rigorous standards are relaxed, and if what purports to be a university honours degree in fact rewards much lower attainments, then that is obviously self-defeating.

If you are not a high flyer ...

If you are not a high-flyer – if you have modest A-level grades or if, as a mature student, you have been advised to think of your local less well-funded university – then maybe you should think more carefully about what exactly you are seeking to do. The ratio of students who drop out – fail to complete their studies – is higher in the less well-funded universities, partly because their facilities are weaker, partly because many of the students they recruit have lower formal qualifications or financial problems. Do think through what you are hoping to achieve. If you simply want to study for its own sake, if you are already reading widely in the subject you have chosen, and if you would value the opportunity to develop your interest in a more structured way under the guidance of specialists, then almost certainly you should find taking a degree course enriching. A mature student who before and after her degree worked in her husband's retail business told me that her three years as a student had been the most rewarding in her life. If you want to study with a specific career in mind, find out what the prospects are, especially given the costs of studying: for example, if you are thinking of going into teaching, ask the admissions tutor before you apply how many of their mature student graduates succeed in gaining employment as teachers in local schools. If you are wondering about embarking on higher education simply because you want to discover yourself, maybe you should be more cautious and realistic. If you know that you are not really very interested in studying, if you put off doing work until deadlines loom, if you do not enjoy reading, if you find reading a scholarly book a slow and difficult business, if you find it hard to follow lectures and to take notes that you can make sense of afterwards, then you ought to pause and reflect on what your best plans might be.

All that raises a large question about higher education policy. There are two views here. One group would say that only the ablest and most committed should go to university, since only they will seize the opportunities fully. Rather than spreading resources painfully thinly, it would be better to fund properly those who would truly benefit, to maintain a smaller number of universities at a higher standard, and to spend the rest of the money on primary and secondary schools. Moreover for many, and especially those I shall describe in Chapter 6, the experience of higher education is a costly distraction.

But the contrary argument has some weight too. While accepting that only a minority of students will be outstanding students, it nonetheless contends that society as a whole benefits if large numbers of people have some experience, however shallow or limited, of university life and teaching, and if that experience is not confined, as it used to be, to a tiny minority. Even 'a smattering of university education spread around is valuable because it alters the general perceptions of a mass of people', in the words of a former tutor of mine, George Holmes, and any widening of learning and culture is therefore beneficial. But you do not need to concern yourself too much with large matters of policy, though it would be useful to be aware of them.

Take a look

Finally, wherever you think of applying, take a look. Before you make your final choices, visit a range of universities. Even if you are restricted to your local area, there may now be more than one university. In England most students who are free to do so choose to go to a university away from their home town, even though there may be a perfectly good university there. Obviously it is cheaper to live and to study at home. But if you do, you will miss out on the typical student experience of living away from your parents with other like-minded young people. And most students choose a university near enough to home to make it possible to go back easily at weekends but not so close that parents are always calling round. Maybe it would have been better if, as in France or Germany, students had normally stayed at home and gone to their nearest university. If you go away to university, you are much less likely to come back to live and work in your home town: one might argue that that contributes to the rootlessness of modern life, and weakens the social and cultural fabric of English provincial cities and of London's suburbs.

But you must deal with the world as it is, and almost certainly you will be intending to leave home. So do choose carefully. Most universities have open days at the end of the summer term for sixth-formers. But it is possible to wander round most universities most of the time. Go in mid-week in term time if you can (for example, during school half-terms: universities do not have half-term breaks), so that you get the feel of the place when it is busy. It is usually possible to go into university libraries without prior warning. And while many university departments will be too busy to help casual callers very much, there is no harm in trying. Exploit any personal contacts. Even once you have made your choices, go to the in-term visit days at as many of the universities that you have applied to as you can afford.

Ask the lecturers about conditions at their universities – ask them who does the teaching (permanent or temporary staff), how large typical classes are, who marks essays and assignments and how long it takes for marked work to be returned, how many hours a week they teach (if they say more than eight to ten beware!), how much time they spend on (wasteful) administration. Ask (i) whether there have been recent rounds of more or less compulsory early retirements, (ii) how many lecturers there are in the department who are in their late fifties and early sixties, (iii) how many young lecturers have been appointed to full-time permanent positions in the last five and the last ten years, and (iv) whether they have been recently affected by internal reorganisations and mergers of departments. The answers to those questions will tell you how pressing the university's financial problems are and how well the particular department is regarded within its institution; in turn that should give you an impression of how good morale is among the lecturers who will be teaching you.

Take a good look round the campus and, if you are not applying to your home university, the town or city in which the university is to be found. After all, as well as studying at the university, you will be living away from home for three years and you will enjoy the experience more if you choose somewhere you will feel at home in.

Chapter 5

How you can benefit from studying at university

When you study at university – when you study any serious subject – you will obviously learn a great deal about that subject. You will become an historian or a physicist or a linguist or whatever, and you will be well-placed to specialise further. If you study medicine, for example, on completing your studies you will be qualified to seek employment as a doctor.

But studying at university does not just deepen your learning in a subject. It also develops your mental powers. For example, if you write a history essay at university, you will need to read relevant books and articles, to understand what they are about, to summarise their arguments, and to select illustrative detail. You will then need to think about the question you have been set, you will need to plan an essay, and then you will have to write it in clear and elegant prose. If it is a class paper, you will then have to be prepared to defend what you have written, justifying your statements, arguing with your teacher, and with fellow students. You may be asked to prepare an assignment with a group of students. If it is an assessed essay, your tutor will mark your written work, but what ought to matter to you is not the mark itself but the comments, in which the tutor will discuss with you the substance of your essay, in particular picking out themes that could be developed and strengthened, and also guiding you on how you could organise your essay better, improve your writing style and so on. As a student you will go through such a process again and again, week by week, month by month, over three years. As a result, because you will have been wrestling with serious and demanding intellectual subjects, guided by researchers in the field, you will not only have learned a great deal about the subject but you will have greatly developed and refined your skills of study.

These skills have recently been set out very eloquently by the History Benchmarking Group, a score of university historians who were invited to do so by the Funding Council's Quality Assurance Agency. In their words, studying history fosters:

- 'a sense of the importance of and distinctiveness of the past, an awareness of the development of differing values, systems and societies';
- 'critical yet tolerant personal attitudes';
- 'the ability to understand how people have existed, acted and thought in the always different context of the past';
- 'the ability to read a text both critically, and empathetically';
- 'the appreciation of the complexity and diversity of situations, events and past mentalities';
- 'the understanding of problems inherent in the historical record itself';
- 'a feeling for the limitations of knowledge and the dangers of over-simplistic explanations';
- 'a recognition that statements are not of equal validity, that there are ways of testing them, and that historians operate by rules of evidence which, though themselves subject to critical evaluation, are also a component of intellectual integrity and maturity';
- 'the ability to set tasks and solve problems';
- 'the ability to gather, sift, select, organise and synthesise large quantities of evidence; the ability to formulate appropriate questions and to provide answers to them using valid and relevant evidence and argument';
- 'an understanding of the nature of the discipline including what questions are currently asked by historians and why'.

The History Benchmarking Group also summarises 'the generic skills acquired through the study of history', namely self-discipline, self-direction, independence of mind and initiative, respect for the reasoned views of others, a capacity to analyse and solve problems, a critical understanding of texts and other media, structure, coherence and fluency of written and oral expression, empathy and imaginative insight, intellectual integrity and maturity. Ideally, that is what you should be acquiring if you study history.

And it is not difficult to see how comparable sets of skills could be set out as the result of studying any rigorous intellectual discipline at university. Here it is necessary to point out that some subjects are more serious than others. They are more difficult and they raise a wider range of issues. Other subjects are less rigorous and consequently less effective at developing your mental skills. Let me stick my head out over the parapet and list the rigorous subjects. My own discipline, history, is undoubtedly rigorous. So are classics and the languages, provided that you study literature in the original language itself, not in translation. Philosophy is a serious and demanding subject. The sciences – physics, chemistry – are rigorous disciplines. So is mathematics. Done properly the study of English literature is serious, but an intellectual catastrophe has fallen upon that field of study in the last generation and you can no longer be sure of how it will be treated. By contrast technical subjects such as management – involving the study of accounting, statistics, marketing – are not as rigorous. There is no substantial body of good work to study in them. However necessary it is to be able to read a balance sheet if you work in business, there is nothing to stretch the mind or to uplift the spirit in learning how to do it. It was interesting that when Lord Weinstock retired as managing director of GEC he declared that universities should only offer degrees in serious subjects such as mathematics, classics and philosophy: business studies, he said, was not in the same league. It is far from clear that studying business studies actually makes you better at business. Then there are newer degrees in media studies, sport management and so forth. Indeed, whenever you think you have invented something quite fantastical, you discover that it is being offered somewhere. But if the purpose of university study is to develop your mental powers, then you have to study something rigorous. Only then will your mind be stretched. It is when you come to grips with a body of learning that you yourself recognise as demanding, that you will feel more and more confident in your ability to take on any intellectual task.

Once you have achieved this kind of intellectual maturity, then you have become what was once called 'educated'. You have developed the intellectual skills that will make it possible for you to turn your hand to virtually anything. And that studying at university greatly develops such intellectual skills is, to be honest, the reason that most students come to university, and the reason that governments fund and expand higher education.

But it is necessary to emphasise here that students deepen and refine their skills by studying the subject they study. You learn by doing. You reflect on the nature of politics in the reign of Henry VIII; you wrestle with the rival interpretations of Anne Boleyn's fall; you decide whether Henry VIII was puppet or puppeteer. You study such questions because they are in themselves interesting and important, and because what has been written on them and is available for you to read is challenging. If you do not go on to become a university historian or a schoolteacher, you are unlikely to use the knowledge you learn directly in the course of your subsequent career. You have not acquired that knowledge 'just in case' it might one day be needed (though conceivably it might), but because in the process of learning about such topics you have developed your mental powers. It is not what you have studied that matters, as Sir Michael Howard has pointed out, but how you have studied it. In learning about such topics and in working out your ideas on such questions you are like an athlete in training, though what you are training is not your body but your mind. And once your mental powers have been developed, then you are prepared – better prepared – to tackle the sorts of tasks characteristic of employment in a wide range of occupations and professions.

You will undoubtedly find that your three years at university will leave an effect on the rest of your life. Much is now being said about 'lifelong learning': but university study has always marked graduates for the rest of their lives. 'Universities', Sir Michael Howard has written, 'should be nuclear reactors. The graduates they send out into the world should be fissile material with a long half-life; certainly one that lasts throughout their professional careers'. What you have been developing is a critical intelligence, and that is an asset that you will use and treasure for the rest of your life.

Does studying at university also make you a better person? Does learning make people good? Does education foster virtue? It was long held that studying the Bible and the great writers of classical literature did indeed promote morality. It made people civilised and cultured. That is now an unfashionable view. 'The idea that the study of humanities makes us morally better is a notion', Sir Keith Thomas has written (*THES* 2 December 1988), 'which most of us would find positively embarrassing'. He went on to cite George Steiner's question about the concentration camp guards who allegedly read Goethe and listened to Mozart yet nonetheless went about their horrible work without compunction. Steiner's question is superficially clever, but it is not based on any empirical study: is it actually generally true? Interestingly, however, Thomas went on to offer a justification for the study of the humanities because 'we know from our own experience how a knowledge of literature and history can help people to lead fuller, richer lives ... they enlarge our experience, enhance our self-consciousness, widen our sense of what is humanly possible, and most important of all, enable us to step outside the assumptions of our own day and to escape the tyranny of present-mindedness'. Thomas was justifying the humanities, and it would not be difficult to elaborate a similar justification for the study at university of any serious subject. As Sir Howard Newby, Chief Executive of the Higher Education Funding Council put it, 'we need to continue to celebrate the purposes of higher education in spreading civilised values'. Studying does not just develop practical skills; it makes you a better person.

Chapter 6

Are too many students like this?

'How many people work in the Vatican?', a pope was once asked by an American President: 'About half' was the reply. In a similar vein, a schoolfriend's father, who was a university professor, would respond to the question 'How many students are there in your department' by saying 'One in three'. Only a minority of students are from the start truly hardworking and determined scholars-in-the-making fired by a passionate desire to diminish their ignorance; a majority do take things very seriously in their third and final year, but not before; a minority never do. Even when there were only around 50,000 university students in total – there are now over a million – Bruce Truscot could declare that in his own experience 'quite 10 per cent, and in some years 20 per cent, are unfitted for university study'.

Most students go to university because it is what is expected of them; because it is what everyone they know does; because their parents want them to; because they think it will lead to a good career; because they think that the social life of a university student, free from parental control, is very enjoyable. Look at the brochures that universities send out and the photographs of life at the university. What you see are pictures of beautiful young people visibly enjoying life – clubbing, listening to music, drinking at the bar, dancing at parties, playing sport, looking dreamily at each other. Parents and their nagging control are nowhere in evidence. Nor is the library or the examination room. Instead the impression is given of a kind of club or holiday camp peopled by large numbers of young people with similar interests enjoyably living together. Those impressions are not false – in many respects that is exactly what student life is like. In their book *Fresher Pressure* (1994), a guide on how to survive as a student, Aidan Macfarlane and Ann McPherson offer chapters on where to live, money, friends, loneliness, sex and relationships, contraception, sexually transmitted diseases, harassment, food, drink and cigarettes, exercise and sport, illegal drugs, then – perhaps not surprisingly – stress and anxiety. But just one of the 20 chapters is about study!

There has always been a lighter side to student life. Rich young men went up to Oxbridge and enjoyed themselves dining and drinking. Up until the nineteenth century the rich did not bother taking examinations and obtaining degrees. Once they did, Oxford offered fourth-class degrees to the idlest of the rich. Sport used to be a central feature of student life at Oxford and Cambridge, as was involvement in political societies and debating societies such as the Oxford Union, and many students gave their studies a lower priority. In the last generation clubbing has become a much more central part of student life. Student unions often run by students with sharp entrepreneurial skills have been able to organise quite lavish and frequent events, and, as student numbers have risen, in most university towns there are now substantial numbers of young people looking to enjoy themselves. For many students, the social life at university, including all their personal relationships, is what matters most to them, and occupies much of their time.

Another increasingly common feature of student life is working for money: often a necessity, though frequently intended to finance lifestyles that include a car and an active social life. If you work for money, you will most likely be doing one of those jobs where what your employer wants is your time and your physical energy – standing and serving at the bar all evening, for example. Because you will be doing something tiring and boring, you will probably feel the need to go out and enjoy yourself afterwards. The risk is that your studies will then take a poor third place.

Many lecturers look on all this with a mixture of disapproval, incomprehension, and sometimes envy for a youthful lifestyle they can no longer enjoy, or perhaps never did. But there is not much that they can do about it. And the best advice that I can give is that you should think clearly about what it is that you want. The downside about partying and all that is associated with it is that, however much you may enjoy the night, the morning after may not be so agreeable. If the hangover came first and the sense of elation did not arrive until the next day, fewer people would drink. If you have a wild night, and if the drugs you take include illegal as well as legal substances, you are unlikely to be at your best for your studies the next day. If you enjoy wild nights several days a week, then you are probably never going to get much academic work done. What makes this terribly unfair is that there are some people who are so tough and so energetic that they can stay up all night doing what they like, and then still work at full power the next day. Sir Geoffrey Elton, the great Tudor historian, apart from chain-smoking untipped Camel cigarettes, would routinely down quantities of malt whisky daily, not to mention pints of beer. After going to bed late, he would regularly rise at 5 a.m., fresh as a daisy, and spend three hours writing every day before breakfast, after which he would start on a normal person's daily round. Not surprisingly a man of such demonic energy achieved much more than the rest of us. Yet he died aged 73 after some years of ill health, relatively young these days, and one can only wonder whether in the long run all that smoking and drinking took its toll in the end. The human body is remarkably resilient and you may feel fine immediately after all sorts of excesses. But sometimes the damage done to the body is cumulative and long-term. One cigarette will do little lasting harm, but 20 cigarettes a day over 40 years probably will. What are your capacities? How much can you take and still feel on top form the next day? No doubt in your late teens you will find out. And most likely you will have to decide your priorities. If you want to do all the work your teachers recommend, then unless you are exceptionally tough you simply will not be able to go out every night.

Many students – probably most students in Years 1 and 2, though somewhat fewer in Year 3 – do not work all that hard. That, of course, is only my impression: it might be that students who appear to be doing very little are in fact working long hours but simply finding their studies difficult and not achieving as much as they should. More reasonably, it might be objected against me that I was an unusually committed student, passionately interested in history, and that it is unfair of me to apply my exceptional enthusiasm as a benchmark against which to judge what most students do. That, however, would seem to concede that my suspicion that the average student does not do all that much is justified.

I do not think that such students deliberately plan to do as little work as they can get away with. I suspect that intentions are often good, but they are not executed. You thought of getting up early to get on with your work – but at the last minute you went to a party last night and you have got up late today and are not feeling too good. You put on the television, even though it is mid-morning. A friend calls and you drink coffee and chat and then it is lunchtime. You plan to go to the library but there is a heavy downpour so you wait and meet another friend. You are then asked at the last minute to make up the numbers for a football match. After tea, you remember you need to buy some toothpaste and coffee so you go to the shops, stop for a drink with friends, by which point it is time for supper. In a fit of virtue, you then settle down at your desk to read, but you feel sleepy and your mind wanders. Loud music wafts into your room from across the way, and then a friend asks you to join in the party ... and so another day passes, enjoyably enough at one level, but with a nagging sense of guilt that no serious work has been done. You have made no plans, or if you have, you have ignored them. True, you have some essay deadlines, but they are a long way off, and the examinations you face are months away. So the next day is much the same ... and then the weekend comes, and you are off to see friends at home or at another university.

And yet it does not seem to matter that much, because you are not being required to do that much work. Take a typical degree course in my subject. In Year 1 you might be doing four courses or 'modules' in each of the two semesters, writing two essays in each course, and then taking an examination in each module in which you will have to answer, say, two questions. Similarly in Year 2, you might now be doing two courses in each semester, and writing two essays per course (though rather longer essays than in Year 1), and facing examinations in each module at the end of the semester. On the face of it all this might seem quite demanding, and indeed most first-year students do see it as a baptism of fire. On paper the courses taken will look ambitious in scope. But in fact writing eight essays (in Year 1) and four essays (in Year 2) in a 12-week semester is not a vast burden, and in some universities the number of essays required may be still smaller.

In the next chapter I shall advise you on how to set about writing essays if you are a committed student who wishes to do well. But if you are not so committed or ambitious, and if you simply want to get by so that you can enjoy your social life, then that, unfortunately, is entirely possible. Look at the reading lists your tutors provide when they set an essay. There are bound to be textbooks that cover the course: choose a recent one. There are many student texts that take a set of events or issues that have been much debated and offer an overview: choose one or two. For example, if you are set an essay on the French wars of religion, look at Richard Bonney, *European Dynastic States*, and R.J. Knecht, *The French Wars of Religion*. Bonney has about 20 pages dealing with the French wars of religion; Knecht's book is wholly devoted to the subject, but it is a short book, and you can pick out relevant sections. What you need to submit is an essay of 2000 words. Be careful not to copy out whole paragraphs, but you can certainly get away with following the rough order and borrowing parts, especially if you give some footnote references to Bonney and Knecht. What you will put together will not be a good essay. It will be a somewhat disorganised mixture of facts and the opinions of Bonney and Knecht, or sometimes Bonney or Knecht quoting other historians' views. And by the time you have finished you will not yourself really know much about the French wars of religion. But your essay will probably get somewhere between 57 and 62 per cent (pass is 40, distinction is 70). It will not have taken you more than a few hours to cobble the essay together, and the mark will be reasonable enough for you to coast towards your next assignment, while taking in several more parties along the way. Of course, you may not do so well in the examination, when you will not have the books to hand. But if you can regurgitate your essays, even if they are not very much to the point or supported by much detail, you are unlikely to go much below 50, unless there are some drastic weaknesses. And since overall marks are now usually a combination of essays and examinations, you will still be surviving comfortably.

Moreover, if what you would like is a II:i degree, all is not lost. Year 1 is a qualifying year: you pass or (very rarely) you fail, and your marks are not carried forward. Year 2 marks do count towards the class of degree – but they are often weighted so that Year 3 marks count for twice as much. If in Year 3 you buckle down and work more seriously, you will have more than a sporting chance of getting your II:i. If you average 63 per cent in Year 3, then only 54 per cent in Year 2 will still produce an average of 60 per cent ($[63 \times 2 + 54 \times 1] \div 3$). So if you choose, you really do not have to work all that hard at all in Years 1 and 2. And most students do not.

Is that a somewhat cynical caricature, terribly unfair? I'm not convinced that students actually plan things with such a degree of calculating precision. I suspect that what I have sketched is not an inaccurate description of what happens, but students rather 'fall into' working like that (or not working very much) because it seems natural. Most students think they are studying very hard. After all, they might say, they have several lectures a week to attend (perhaps eight a week in Year 1, four a week in Year 2) and a number of classes (perhaps one a fortnight in each of their courses in Year 1, one a week in each of their courses in Year 2). They might be asked to prepare short reports to start off discussion in one of the classes on each of their courses. And when you have a lecture at 11 o'clock and a class at 3 o'clock, it is somehow hard to get to the library to do anything useful before the lecture, or after the lecture and before lunch, or after lunch and before the class … Essay deadlines come all too quickly, the books are not in the library just when you need them, and your essay is put together in a great rush. Things change in Year 3: one of my third-year students last year commented in an anonymous questionnaire that the work expected – and achieved – in Year 3 was as much as that in Years 1 and 2 put together.

Why are university students allowed to work so little in Years 1 and 2? Part of the answer is that universities have been designed with the best students in mind. Committed students burning with zeal to learn all they can about their subjects want simply to be given the greatest opportunities to get on with it. All they need is an assignment and a reading list and they will do all that is asked and more. Part of the answer reflects the attitudes of lecturers. They are, or at least they once were, idealistically committed to their studies, and they do not think it their role to motivate uncommitted students to study when they do not much want to.

A more important recent explanation is that this reflects contemporary educational ideologies. Educationalists and many politicians have a horror of 'exclusion'. They do not wish to set standards that 'exclude' people. So in universities what is required has been reduced to reflect what the average student actually does. A recent guide for lecturers suggests that they set deadlines for the submission of essays on Tuesdays at 4 p.m., so that students weekending away can return on Monday.

Still more important is the fact of underfunded expansion. The main reason why first- and second-year students are set little work to do is that there are increasingly large numbers of them and no more of us. We simply could not cope with the marking load if we set our students more essays to write. We are researchers as well as teachers: unlike schoolteachers, only part of our time can be spent teaching and marking. So we have cut back remorselessly on what students are asked to do.

Of course, if you are working – or not working – like this, then not only will you not be learning very much of the subject that you are supposedly studying, but you will not be acquiring and refining those mental skills that we were considering in the previous chapter, you will not be developing a critical intelligence, and to that extent your experience of university life will be impoverished. You may be enjoying yourself; you may have gone to university simply because everyone does; you may have vague expectations that your university degree will get you a better job; you will undoubtedly absorb something from your years at university, and perhaps towards the end you will at last begin to get a taste of what it all ought to have been about. But if you are not really interested in your subject or committed enough to study hard, then you ought to think twice about what you are doing. What you make of university is very much up to you: but you should begin by being aware of what the choices are.

Part III

How to make the most of your studies

In Chapter 6 we met students who just coast through their studies while enjoying student social life. In Part III of this book I shall revert to my idealistic mode and assume that you are ambitious and hard-working, but that you are anxious about just how to organise your studies to make them as effective and as productive as they can be. There are no magic tips for studying effectively, no theories that guarantee the highest success; tips are all low-level stuff, and open to dispute; but nonetheless it is useful to stand back and think about what you are doing.

Students are far from equal in talents, ambition and commitment, so it is impossible to offer advice like this without, for some of the time at least, irritating you. If you are already successful and confident in your studies, you may well find what follows obvious and patronising – or you may think it simply wrong. What you might profitably do, however, is to try to set out yourself why you think your studying has gone well, and what advice you would give to those younger than you are now. Clearly much of what follows is pitched at the student who is eager but a little unsure of exactly what is expected, who knows more or less what to do, but is keen to be assured that he or she is on the right lines. I have also offered more demanding suggestions, intended specially for the more ambitious students who are aiming at a first-class degree. My advice reflects my own experience as an historian and as a teacher of history students, and I cite my own experiences for illustration, but much of what I suggest applies in much the same way in the humanities and social sciences and, in broad terms, in all subjects.

Chapter 7

Getting started

You have been made a conditional offer of a place at university. Apart from making sure you meet the grades demanded, what next?

The most important practical matter is accommodation. Many universities automatically offer new students a room in a hall of residence. My strong advice is to accept. Of course, not all student accommodation is wonderful; some is pretty basic or greatly in need of refurbishment, but most is at least adequate, and some rather good. Ask the students whom you meet when you go on a visit-day which halls of residence they would recommend. Living in halls may be a little more expensive than the alternatives. But it is worth it. The great advantage of starting off in a hall of residence is that you are bound to meet a great many students, especially if you are in a hall in which evening meals are provided. If you are not offered a place in halls, your university should have lists of rooms, flats and houses available to rent: badger the accommodation office. It can be rather dispiriting looking for somewhere to live: do not let it get you down. If your parents can afford to buy you a flat or house that has obvious advantages. And many students, especially mature students, live at home. But remember that if you do not begin in a hall of residence, you will have to make more of an effort to meet other students.

Sort out your finances. Find out what you will need to pay. In 1998 the New Labour Government introduced what it misleadingly called a tuition fee of £1000 to be paid each year by university students. It has been increased annually: the rate for 2002–03 in England and Wales has been set at £1100. There are exemptions. If your parents' income (and the calculations for this are quite complex) is less than £20,480, then you will not need to pay anything; if your parents' income is between £20,480 and £30,502, then you will be exempt from a proportion of the fee; but if your parents' income is over £30,502 then you must pay it in full. In Scotland, since 2001–02 new students have no longer been required to pay annual tuition fees, but instead face a Graduate Endowment, set initially at £2000, when they complete their studies.

You will also need to take out a loan from the Student Loans Company in order to cover your living expenses while you are studying. In 1998 the New Labour Government abolished the system of student grants. Instead, the sums (means-tested against their parents' income) previously given to students as grants have now been turned into loans. The Student Loans Company will for 2002–03 lend a maximum of £3090 to students who live at home, £3905 to students who live away from home, and £4815 to students in London. All students are entitled to borrow 75 per cent of these sums; students whose parental incomes are below £30,502 may borrow a greater proportion. In order to take out a loan, you will need to apply to your Local Education Authority (in your home town, and not where you will be studying). You will need to fill in a form before mid-March (look for it on your LEA website; per-haps your school or college will have copies) to demonstrate your eligibility, and then you will be sent another form on which your par-ents will be required by mid-June to give details of their income. Once your LEA has sorted out your entitlement, you will then be able to apply to the Student Loans Company for a loan. As you can see, it is a cum-bersome business. And there are bizarre variations: if you live in Birmingham, Hampshire, Waltham Forest, East Sussex or Wiltshire, you must do everything on a single form. It is prudent to begin applying as soon as you receive a conditional place.

You will not need to repay the loans that you take out from the Student Loans Company until you earn over £833 a month or £192 a week (or roughly £10,000 a year), but interest will be calculated and added to the loan from the start. The rate of interest is simply the rate of retail price inflation, set once a year: in 2001–02 it was 2.3 per cent, in 2002–03 1.3 per cent. You will therefore pay back exactly what you bor-row adjusted for inflation. Once you start earning, you will pay back 9 per cent of whatever you earn over £10,000 a year. The calculations are complex, but if you earn £20,000 you will pay £75 a month. You will go on paying this until all you owe is repaid. Just how long it will take to repay the loan will depend on future rates of inflation, and it is not dif-ficult to imagine significant problems if the rate of inflation again rises to 10 per cent. You can repay the loan in full at any time. In many ways this system helps the better-off. If your parents can afford to support you through university, you can borrow the maximum amount and invest it in a building society: the difference between the interest you are charged on the loan and the interest you are paid provides a small but welcome additional income.

Unless your parents are well-off and generous, you will now almost certainly end your years at university substantially in debt to the Student Loans Company and, quite likely, to your bank. It is worth noting here that the maximum sums that you are allowed to borrow from the Student Loans Company fall a good way short of what you will need. You may think it remarkable that a government that claims to be committed to widening and extending access to higher education should have introduced tuition fees and abolished grants. Students from poorer backgrounds face real problems. There are often practical complications – delays in processing forms can mean that loan cheques are delayed. It is true that there are various complex schemes that offer some help. Mature students do not have to pay tuition fees. There are access bursaries for students with children (though the terms scarcely seem generous). A recent initiative in England and Wales offers 8000 bursaries worth £2000 each to students in certain schools and colleges who come from families in which there is little or no experience of higher education. But the number of bursaries is tiny compared to the total number of students. Scotland, as often, is more generous, and non-repayable bursaries worth £2050 are available to all students from low-income families (defined as a residual family income of £26,000). But even £2000 or £2050 are far from sufficient to meet the standard living costs. The rules of entitlement to such schemes are numbingly complex (see the official guide, *Financial Support for Higher Education Students in 2002/03*) and may often seem unfair. And it is often those just above the thresholds that seem most harshly treated by the current system: not poor enough to receive bursaries, but not affluent enough to pay without pain. Universities administer hardship funds designed to assist in difficult circumstances, but the sums they can afford to provide are small. I wish that I could be more encouraging to would-be students who are not well-off: perhaps reforms will come. Do not hesitate to ask for guidance and help in advance: both your Local Education Authority and the university which has accepted you ought to be able to give you advice on financial matters.

And as soon as you have received a cheque from the Student Loans Company (or, if you are fortunate enough to receive a bursary, from your Local Education Authority), open a bank account if you do not already have one. Remember, however, that banks are profit-making commercial organisations, and be careful about any further borrowing. Before entering into any financial commitments, take plenty of advice. Don't forget to insure your possessions before you go up to university, especially if you have a computer or expensive electronic equipment.

You will undoubtedly wonder at times whether you ought to be doing some preparation, especially during the summer vacation immediately before you go up. You may be given some specific tasks, in which case there is no problem. More generally, however, it is not easy to prepare for courses in advance, since you will have little guidance at this stage, and whatever you do may well turn out to be inappropriate.

My advice would be to approach your studies in the round and do what would offer a useful springboard in general. For example, if you are going to study English literature, you can be fairly certain that at some point you will be reading some of Shakespeare's plays. Why not set out to read as many as you can before you come up? Similarly, it is quite likely that you will be studying George Eliot and Charles Dickens. No doubt in the specific courses you take you will concentrate on one or two of their novels. But why not read as many as you can in the summer vacation before you come up? Of course, these are ambitious targets and if you get anywhere near them, then you are the kind of student who is heading towards a first-class degree. But even if you read just two or three plays and novels over and above what you have already done at school you will undoubtedly find it very useful.

If you are going to study history, it is harder to make such suggestions, since you are likely to specialise, and there are few topics that every student studies. But why not give yourself an architectural background to your historical studies? Visit a Norman castle, a medieval cathedral, a late medieval manor house, a perpendicular-style parish church, a Tudor merchant's house, a classical country house, a Victorian church, a Victorian town hall, and so on, so that whatever period you come to be studying, you can add to your studies an architectural dimension.

In the weeks just before you begin, rather than nervously fretting about what it will all be like, develop (or acquire) some practical skills. Can you cook? You will almost certainly spend some of your years at university in self-catering accommodation. Boiling vegetables, frying, grilling or stewing meat is not so difficult, and cooking for yourself is certainly cheaper and healthier than relying on junk food. Can you do your own laundry? Once again, washing and ironing is really not that difficult, however much more agreeable it is to be doing something else.

The weeks immediately before you go up are a good time to talk to anyone you know who is already a student or who has recently gradu-ated: those – such as your parents – whose experience of university goes back twenty years or more may not be able to give you such up-to-date guidance.

Once you arrive at your chosen university you will find a large number of activities laid on for you, from the long queues at registration, through introductory lectures and parties, to meetings of a range of clubs and societies. Do go along to as many as you can, especially if you have some special enthusiasms or talents, but also if you are just intrigued. If you are good at sport, join a team; if you play a musical instrument, join an orchestra; if you are interested in politics, join the student association. But do not just turn up; offer to help. Above all, do not spend the first week at university sitting on your own in your room. In some universities, it is true, you will be set demanding academic work at once. In most universities, however, you will find that your first assignments are not due for three or four weeks – and while that should not mislead you about the amount of work and effort that studying at university demands, it does obviously give you time to settle in and to get to know your fellow students.

And that really is the key to enjoying your years at university. Many students make friends for life. Do not be shy introducing yourself to other students whenever you find yourself sitting together at dinner or queueing at registration. When a lecture or class is over, ask the student next to you to join you for coffee or for lunch, and do not be put out if, for whatever reason, the answer is no, or not just now. Tell other students where you come from, what you are studying. Share with them your impressions of your hall of residence or of your first lectures and classes. Do not be put off if other students appear more confident, more at ease, more knowledgeable than you. Almost always they feel just the same as you do, even if they look more confident. And, if they are indeed more clued-up than you, do not let that bother you, but flatter them by asking for advice and help (but remember you do not have to take it, and never do anything you do not want to). Almost always new students do get to know lots of other students – and with luck a few will become really good friends.

If you feel unhappy in your first weeks, try to work out why. If you are feeling uncertain about your studies, keep reading through this book: the next chapters are intended to demystify what is involved in studying at university. If you think you have chosen the wrong course, do not hesitate to talk it through with your tutors and see if it is possible to switch (it often is, but the sooner the better). Do not be too hasty to give up altogether. It is normal to feel moments of doubt, to do less well than you hoped, to feel lonely, but most students quickly bounce back.

If something of this sort is bothering you a useful technique is to promise yourself that you will think seriously about it a week from now, but that you will try not to worry about it all before then. Very likely what seems a mountainous problem will have disappeared by then and you may even forget to think about it. And remember that overwhelmingly, students enjoy their years at university, finding them rewarding both intellectually and socially.

Chapter 8

Routines of study

What will almost certainly be different from your life at school (though perhaps less so if you have been at college) is that you will have far fewer formal classes and lectures. That is less true in the sciences and engineering and medicine, where it is common for mornings to be spent in lectures and afternoons in the laboratory (or the other way about). In the arts and social sciences, however, you will probably have no more than ten hours of lectures and classes in Year 1, and quite possibly five or six hours in Year 3: at Oxford and Cambridge your only commitment might be one tutorial a week. After the experience of school, where you are told what you will be doing at every point in the week, it can come as quite a shock to have so much time that is not ordered for you.

And it may also be a surprise that, unlike at school, at university if you do not turn up for classes or if you fail to submit an essay, it may take some time before anyone (perhaps the Student Loans Company) notices your absence or your idleness and reproaches you. At school you may have had as many as six periods a week with the same subject teacher and work to prepare every week. At university, you might have a fortnightly class with each of your lecturers, so it will take a while before lecturers know who you are, especially if the class is large. The first deadlines for written work on each course can be several weeks into term, so that if you are not studying, it will be a while before it is noticed. University lecturers pay you the compliment of treating you as adults, and as serious and committed students: they trust you to get on with what you are expected to do, without any reminders that your work is due in on a specified date. If you break that trust, and do not even do the minimum that I was describing in the previous chapter, you may feel clever for a time to be getting away scot-free with doing nothing, but your lack of effort will eventually expose you, and by then it may be very difficult to make up for lost time.

The most important tasks that you will have to do are the essays or problems or other assignments that you are set by your lecturers. *Organise your daily routine to give yourself plenty of time to do whatever assignments you are set* (and make sure you find out early on exactly what these are). If you are required to write an essay a week (as at Oxford), that is straightforward, and you embark on a regular cycle of work. But if you are set, say, four or eight essays to write in a semester with various submission dates, you need to do some planning. If it helps, write the important dates down in your diary, or buy a wall-planner and keep it somewhere that you will see it every day, or use computer software. It does not matter how you do this, but you will find it invaluable to be aware of and in control of your schedule of assignments.

Make sure that you allow yourself plenty of time in the library or at home with the books and articles you need to read. It may be sensible to work at the essays in turn, but take care not to spend a disproportionate amount of time on one of them at the cost of rushing the rest. Do not leave everything to the last possible moment; you will find it difficult to get hold of the books you need, and consequently you will not do as well.

Remember that the purpose of study is to master a subject. So the answer to the general questions, 'How many hours should I work?', 'How many books should I read?', is simply 'As much and as many as you need to feel that you have mastered the subject'. It is not, unfortunately, enough to set yourself a set number of hours to work or pages to read. Academic study is not a mechanical exercise like mowing a lawn. The danger of setting yourself such numerical targets is that you will simply perform them mechanically, sitting in the library for so many hours, but in fact daydreaming for many of them. What counts is mastering the subject you are studying. True, to do that you will need to put in the hours, so setting yourself targets of hours to work or pages to read can be a useful way to plan your time, but clocking up that set number of hours' work or reading that fixed number of pages is not in itself the point.

As a rough guide remember that anyone employed in an office job will be expected to work 35–40 hours a week. If you had not gone to university, that is what would have been expected from you in the kind of employment you would most likely have taken. That is not an unreasonable target for you: it amounts (for example) to seven or eight hours a day Monday to Friday, leaving weekends free. Add up your lectures and classes, take the total from 40: ask yourself if you are spending that much on your reading and preparation of assignments. If you are not, then perhaps you are not working hard enough … (have you by chance escaped from Chapter 6?). What makes this an awkward model to follow is that studying at university is not like a nine-to-five clerical job. It is very probable that your assignment deadlines will be bunched towards the end of a term or semester, so there may well be some weeks when you hardly have any time to spare. Similarly, you are likely to be revising very intensively in the period just before examinations.

Make sure that you leave plenty of uninterrupted time to study. Set aside a whole morning or afternoon or evening for concentrated study, reading or writing for two or three hours at a stretch. Do that several times a week (to get up to a total of forty hours a week including all your lectures and classes), and you will soon have a sense of achievement.

If you are better in the mornings than in the evenings, try to plan the most important studying you do then; if you are at your intellectual best late at night, write your essays into the small hours.

Decide where you study best: some students like to work in their own room, others concentrate best in the library, sitting in exactly the same place every day, surrounded by others who are reading. If you work best when everything is quiet, then you may well be better off borrowing books and taking them home, provided that your family or your flatmates do not spoil your concentration.

Avoid anything that might distract you. Professor Wernham, historian of Tudor foreign policy, lived in a house on the coast with a wonderful view across the Solent to Ryde and the Isle of Wight; for his study, however, he used a room that looked out onto the road away from the sea. If you work regularly at home, try to make your environment as conducive to study as you can: good lighting, a desk that does not wobble, a good chair and so on.

But realise that life is full of petty frustrations – the bus is late, the train breaks down, the computer will not work, the book you want in the library is being read by someone else, the boiler has broken down, the neighbours are playing loud music – and rise above them. *Get on with it.* Set yourself a time to start, and start. Put everything else out of your mind for the time being. Do not wait for perfect conditions. Like going for a country walk, you may be sluggish to start with, but once you have been striding out for some time, you find your rhythm and can press on productively.

When you stop studying for the day – whether because it is late in the night, or because you are going out for the evening, or because you are now going to classes, or whether you simply feel you have had enough – *before you stop, make a brief note of what you are going to do next* – what reading you are going to do next, what aspect of a topic you are going to explore next, so that when you return to it, instead of floundering and trying to remember where you had got to, you can make a flying start. This is especially worthwhile if you are studying several different courses in the same term and if, consequently, it may be several days before you can come back to what you have just stopped doing.

Try to make time for your studies by saving time on chores. Remember Parkinson's Law: work expands to fill the time available for its completion. An elderly aunt manages to spend a whole day sending a gift to her nephew, searching first for writing paper, then for her pen, then mislaying her glasses, then going out to buy a stamp, then coming home and finding she has run out of envelopes, and so on. By contrast her nephew writes a letter of thanks in a matter of seconds. Use idle moments to catch up on routine correspondence; to pay bills; pop into the library between classes to order books or check references; try to plan your shopping ahead; do not let your dirty laundry pile up ... Maximise the time you have free for serious work.

Plan ahead to allow time for socialising. Keep ahead of your schedule so that if something unexpected turns up – an invitation to what is likely to be a particularly good party or dinner or film or a day at the races, or whatever, you can go along without having to skimp on your work. Plan ahead to allow for the less pleasant experience of being out of action with a heavy cold for a few days.

Remember that it is up to you to organise your time, to structure your day, your week, your term: no lecturer will do it for you.

Try keeping a diary to see exactly where your time is going. Plot the days of the week across the top and the hours of the day down the side and enter the lectures/classes you attend, the hours you spend reading, writing essays, doing chores, playing sport, messing around, going out ... It can be revealing to know just how many (or just how few) hours you spend studying.

Perhaps you feel that advice to organise your time better is misplaced because you are simply not the kind of person who can operate in that way: you are spontaneous, intuitive, and you can only work well when you are really committed, and not to order. I am somewhat sceptical, since any human existence requires a degree of self-organisation to function at all, unless you are more or less totally dependent on others. And if this is how you feel, be prepared for difficulties as deadlines for the submission of work loom. Do you always write your essays at the very last possible moment? If you do, and if you feel rushed, and wish while doing them that you had started earlier, and resolve not to leave it so late next time, then you ought to think very carefully about working to a better plan. If, however, you leave your essays as long as possible but always get what you aim at done, if you feel that the pressure of leaving yourself limited time to write the essay actually helps you concentrate, focuses your efforts, then fine – but you might concede that you are in fact rather well organised, in that you have developed working methods that suit your personality rather well.

When you begin, and again when you begin each new year or semester, *get a rough sense of what the courses you are taking involve*. These days you are likely to be given a handbook and the courses will have lists of 'aims' and 'objectives' and, more helpfully, lists of the topics you will be covering: if not, make sure you have an idea of what is coming, and see how the parts of a course relate to the whole week by week. Some lecturers are not well organised, so if you and your fellow students feel a few weeks into a course that you do not have a clear sense of the direction the course is taking, do not be shy to ask the lecturer to explain, and if that does not help, do not hesitate to discuss it with your personal tutor. And if there are any particular topics that are not being covered which you think should be, do not hesitate to ask the lecturer about them. Again, be on the lookout if the lecturer does not seem to be keeping up with the planned syllabus; if it looks as if several scheduled topics are not going to be reached, or if the last part of the syllabus is squashed into a hurried last lecture, then ask, and check that any examination will be testing you fairly on what the course has covered. In fact, you are unlikely to need to worry too much, since you ought still to have sufficient knowledge for the examination, and perhaps the fault lies with an over-ambitious syllabus rather than with anything the lecturer is doing.

Make sure you receive all the materials being distributed: handbooks, essay titles, reading lists. Check with your fellow students. If you lose a reading list, ask friends if you can photocopy theirs. Increasingly lecturers put such information on their webpages: check these too.

You will need to make plenty of use of your university library. No doubt there will be introductory courses, and these are useful, though it is not always easy to absorb a great deal of instructional information. Library computer systems can be capricious. So plan to spend a couple of hours, early on in your time at university, just wandering around the library. Go at a quiet time, perhaps in the evening. Begin with where the books in your subject are shelved, and try to grasp the rough arrangement of books. Look where the periodicals in your subject are kept – both the unbound new issues, and the bound old volumes (they are likely to be in different places). Then look for subjects related to your own, and then just explore, looking to see what is where. If something interesting catches your attention, browse.

If you need practical help with your courses – if something seems odd, if you think you may not be doing the right number of courses, if there is a timetable clash – the best place to go is the departmental office. The administrators and secretaries will have a stock of knowledge on which to draw, and they will be able to help. But remember that they are busy and that there may be certain times of day (lunchtimes for example) when they are not available.

Do not expect everything to be easy or straightforward. After all, the problems you will be wrestling with are likely to have occupied scholars for much of their lives. *Substantial academic books demand your total attention over many hours, even days.* To read them you will have to detach yourself from the pressures of daily life. You will have to read on, rather than worrying about the shopping or the laundry or dinner. You will have to press on, rather than watching television, going to the football or joining your friends in the pub. It is this that gives universities their 'ivory tower' and unworldly image.

Serious academic subjects do not always yield up their treasures quickly. Some issues are necessarily technical and not usefully simplified. Do not expect to feel that you are on top of everything at once; just as footballers or opera singers have to do a great deal of routine and tedious training and practice, so you may have to do a good deal of basic work before you know enough to make your studies exciting. If you are studying a language, French for example, then you simply have got to know French vocabulary: there is no way round that. But the more you do, the more you will come to feel in control. Do not worry, and above all, do not panic if you feel as if you are walking in thick fog: the mists will lift. Try to set down what you do think you know – and try to write down what you do not feel you have understood: the effort will itself help you understand it better. Remember that the point of all education is to stretch you, to challenge you to do a bit more, every time, than you have done before, to learn about things you do not yet know much about, to go deeper than you have gone before.

Avoid too much comparison with other students. *Do not think that everyone is more intelligent or knows more than you.* Remember that you may well not have a full picture. The blasé student who never seems to study but does rather well is almost certainly disguising how much work he – it almost always is a he – is actually doing in an attempt to appear effortlessly brilliant. The student who talks so loudly in class may well not be producing essays that match his or her confidence. But even if you are sure that some of your fellow students are doing better than you, so what? Their record has nothing whatsoever to do with how much *you* can learn, provided you work away at your studies.

But do discuss the courses you are taking and your ways of studying with your fellow students. Think about what you are doing and about how your colleagues may be doing things differently, and see whether you have anything to learn from them.

Try to take pleasure in the successes of others, even if these are successes that you would have liked to have achieved. Delight in something done superbly well – and do not think that you are diminished because you have not done it too. Maybe you will in time.

Be aware, if you are a hard-working and successful student, that you risk provoking the jealousy of others. Dislike of the 'tall poppies' is a depressing feature of human life and it is not easy to avoid or to cope with. It is curious that successful footballers or cricketers are admired as heroes, yet successful students are derided as 'swots', 'brainboxes', 'teacher's pets', 'too clever by half', 'boffins'. Deliberately working less or more slowly, or appearing less knowledgeable and intelligent than you are (simply not to upset your colleagues) worsens things in general, is not going to make you feel happier, and is unlikely to work: you will inadvertently reveal your superior intelligence at some point. You can try to appear effortlessly brilliant – in the hope that if your success rests on what you were born with rather than on your own efforts, it might more easily be accepted by your peers. But academic success at the highest level is very hard to achieve except by putting in the hours at the reading or in the laboratory, so unless you are going to get up at 4 a.m., when everyone else is asleep, to get on with your studies, this is not a realistic option. Clearly it helps not to boast of how hard you are working, how many hours you are studying, how many pages of how many books you have read, or how high the marks you have received have been. If you are a brilliant student, try to put yourself in the shoes of your less able and studious peers, and (hard though it can be to do this without seeming patronising) do not assume that they are as clever and hard-working as you. But the best advice must surely be to be yourself, rather than pulling your punches and achieving less than you are capable of.

Do not worry unnecessarily if you lose time because you are ill. You are bound to have coughs and colds or 'flu; you may be unlucky enough to injure yourself or (much less often) to suffer some more serious illness. Let your tutors know if you miss a class through illness; extensions are readily given on medical grounds. If you are out of action for more than a week, get a medical certificate from your doctor and send it to your personal tutor. Your troubles will then be taken into account by examination boards and you can be assured that you will not be penalised. Do not worry if you have to miss lectures and classes. Ask the teachers concerned once you have recovered if you have missed anything essential and what you should do about it. In most humanities and social science subjects, missing a lecture or class or two will not damage you. You are not going to be tested to see if you have done 100 per cent of your syllabus, so you can afford to miss a bit. But it is a sensible insurance policy to build into your planning the possibility that you may lose a few days through illness.

Chapter 9

Lectures and lecturers

My emphasis here so far has been on your reading and thinking as students. It is likely that you will in addition have had the chance to hear lectures on the subjects on which you are preparing essays and assignments. Lectures are a very characteristic feature of university life. They usually last 45–50 minutes. It may be an unfamiliar experience for you to sit listening to anyone talking for so long. Most television and radio programmes are broken up into much shorter sections. Politicians and preachers do speak for longer, but how often have you been to a political rally or to a sermon in a church? Perhaps you have been to a talk by a visiting speaker at a local society. Or maybe you have been to a conference at which university lecturers were guest speakers. Lectures are so common in university teaching that you will soon get used to them.

Lectures were a central feature of the earliest universities in the middle ages. The word is derived from the Latin for 'reading', and at first lectures were readings by the teacher – or lecturer – from his notebook. In a world without printing, the typical student could not go out and buy a copy of, say, Aristotle. Instead he went to a lecture and took down his teacher's version of Aristotle's text, together with his commentary on it. Such lectures were more like dictations. With the invention and spreading of printing in the fifteenth century, lectures as dictations of scarce texts lost their point, but they survived in a different form.

Here there is a difference between students in arts and social science subjects on the one hand and the physical sciences on the other. Scientists use lectures to convey and to explain a great deal of up-dated information that is often difficult or very hard work to obtain otherwise, and in some respects their lectures are comparable to medieval lectures. In arts and social sciences subjects, lectures serve a rather different function, and are best treated as just another article or chapter in a book. If they are good – if the lecturer is giving you the fruits of his or her research – they will be invaluable and exciting. There is an immediacy in hearing a lecture that makes its impact greater, usually, than that of a book. But lectures are not intended to tell you all you need to know, and they are certainly not intended to tell you 'the answers'. Lectures are often not compulsory, and it is for you to judge whether lectures are useful or not. Maybe the time would be better spent in the library.

Lectures are a very cost-effective way of disseminating knowledge and ideas. A single lecturer can speak to as many students as the lecture theatre can hold, but obviously a lecture has to be tailored to the average student, and cannot therefore address the particular needs of all of them. Consequently some students will sometimes find that lecturers assume they already know a good deal, while at other times feel that a lecturer is simply telling them the basics. Most lecturers have a lot to say, and in pitching their lectures, they usually have in mind the sort of hardworking student that they once were. If you find lectures hard to follow, it might be worth trying some background reading on the subject first, week by week. Lecturers often think you already know the basic outlines and would be bored or feel patronised if they went through them. They will lecture on, say, the First World War, assuming you know exactly when it took place, between whom, and in what ways, and thinking that you would feel insulted and treated like ignoramuses if they first told you that it broke out in 1914: they focus instead on the latest controversies, arguing passionately against their academic rivals. Ideally a lecturer would quickly convey the essentials, without letting it take up too much time, perhaps weaving them into the more important points to be made.

But not all lecturers are ideal lecturers. The way a lecture is presented reflects the personality of the lecturer. Since it is very difficult to change anyone's personality, I very much doubt that there is much that can be done, for example through training courses, to improve the presentation of lectures. Of course, what really matters to you as a student is the content of the lecture – the information, the ideas. It is nice if you are entertained by a lecture, but what you really want is not a theatrical display of pyrotechnics but something substantial that will help you in your studies. For my part, I am prepared to put up with poor delivery, much though I regret it, if a lecture is full of interesting ideas. Gilbert Highet, in his classic book *The Art of Teaching*, declared that the single most important requirement for a teacher is to know the subject that he or she is teaching. And by that, Highet did not mean simply having got up just enough to get through today's lecture, but being thoroughly in command of the subject, fully aware of the latest developments.

From your point of view as a student, it is useful to study the different lecturing styles of lecturers, since that will help you make the best of their lectures. I like lecturers who vary the pace at which they speak, going quickly through illustrative examples, but much more slowly when they emphasise the main points they are making, and pausing between sections. I like lecturers who look at their audience, making eye contact, try to gauge reactions, and adjust their lecture on their feet. But not everyone can do this (you have to have good eyesight). Some people talk to everyone they meet in the same way, while others are much more sensitive, adjusting their language and what they say depending on whether they are talking to their colleagues or to a child or to a friendly but uneducated neighbour. Some lecturers may speak too fast (so that you cannot follow them), or too slowly (so your mind wanders) all the way through, without any variation of pace. Some may swallow the last word in a sentence (so that it is very difficult to keep up with their train of thought), or stop, and 'er', several times in a sentence: to err is human, to go on erring is hellish. Some may speak too quietly: it is worth calling out politely, 'Could you speak louder, please!', though unfortunately some lecturers are very softly spoken and there is not much they can do, in the absence of amplification, to project their voices. (Curiously, it is very unusual for lecturers to be offered training in voice-projection.) In some lecture theatres the acoustics are very bad: sit as close to the front as you can.

These days lecturers often have so much teaching and administration to do, and are being harried to publish as well, that they give their greatest attention to the content of their lectures – their arguments, their evidence – rather than to what they see as the more superficial matter of presentation. Ideally a lecturer would try out a lecture at home or with friends, several times, checking the time each section takes to present, rewriting passages that seem less clear, marking some passages for special emphasis, trying to make notes from the lecture to gauge how students would respond to them, and getting to know the lecture very well. In the real world there is no time for that.

Remember that when, for example, you see a television programme immaculately presented, the presenter has not written everything alone but has been working with a team of assistants; the programme has been rehearsed again and again under the direction of a producer; and even if it only lasts half an hour, much of the working week of a dozen or more assistants may have been devoted to the making of just that half an hour. By contrast a lecturer in a typical week might be taking several classes on different subjects as well as giving not just one but two or three or four lectures (not to mention administrative duties and getting on with his or her publishing, and all that with little, if any, assistance): it just would not be possible to give the time to the presentation of a lecture that producers and their teams give to the presentation of their television programmes. On the other hand most television presenters and their staff are not experts in the subjects they talk about: they spend lots of time on presentation, but the content of the programmes they make is much more superficial and usually dependent on buying the expertise of specialists, often university teachers …

Lecturers tend to be most worried – strange though it may seem to you – that there might be someone in the audience who knows more about their topic than they do and could catch them out. So they are very cautious and tentative, they go into great detail, they consider every possible objection to their claims, they suddenly hesitate as another difficulty occurs to them while they are speaking. They want to get it right, but they are not yet convinced that they have, and so they will not commit themselves definitely, and they will not want to speak too forcefully, too boldly, too clearly, because if they did they would not be true to themselves. A good student who is well-prepared and interested will still find such lectures very helpful, for all their uncertainty in delivery, because they reveal a scholar grappling with his or her subject. But a less committed student who comes to the lecture with little prior knowledge of the subject may well end up confused and bored.

Some lecturers have so much to say that they do not want to waste time by repeating and summarising. By the halfway point they are worried that they will not get through everything, so they rush on, with the consequence that if your mind wanders to what you were doing last night you will not only miss what the lecturer is saying at that moment but lose the thread altogether.

Lecturers usually reuse their lectures, rewriting a proportion each year, and adjusting and amending others in response to their own research and the publications of others. But in an imperfect world there is not always time to look over last year's lectures or to rearrange them beforehand: some confident and articulate lecturers rework their lectures on their feet, in front of their audience: sometimes it works well; sometimes it can get a bit muddled.

Some lecturers read out a complete text. Others talk from just a page of notes. A few talk without any notes at all. Some lecturers like to have a text or notes, but to look up frequently to gauge the reactions of their audience, and talk ad lib. Study the methods of your lecturers – which works best? Are lectures based on full texts the most useful, because they are full and clearly structured? Or are they boring, lacking in drama? Do lecturers who break off from their text to ad lib keep your interest better, or do they risk losing the structure of the lecture, giving too much time to a single example or part of a topic and then having to rush the rest? Are lecturers who speak not from a full text but improvise from a page of notes more lively? Or are lecturers who speak without any notes at all the best because everything seems so completely spontaneous, as if they have only just thought everything out in the presence of the class – or are lecturers who try to do this like cyclists who shout 'look no hands' before falling off? Do their lectures contain too little detailed information to be useful, are they just a superficial show, do they end up rambling all over, and are their apparently spontaneous performances actually a bit of a con because in fact they have been carefully rehearsed?

Thinking about lecturing styles will help you make the most of your lectures. Few lecturers are perfect and you may well have to fill in the gaps one way or another. Above all you will have to learn to concentrate, however difficult a lecturer makes it, and, if necessary, to come to a lecture prepared.

Some lecture courses are deliberately and clearly designed to cover the syllabus. That is straightforward. But other sets of lectures – and they may be very valuable indeed – quite deliberately concentrate on a number of themes in the syllabus, perhaps those reflecting the lecturer's current research interests, rather than on uniform or blanket coverage. Lecturers who do that usually make it clear what their purpose is. When they do not, it can be very confusing until you realise what they are doing. A distinguished historian gave a set of lectures in my first term as a student under the series title 'Gibbon and Macaulay'. Gibbon and Macaulay were two historians whose books we were studying as set texts, so we all went along to the lectures. They were stylishly written, interesting in themselves – but very puzzling because they were about neither Gibbon nor Macaulay but about other historians and ways of writing history. Only much later did I grasp that the lecturer had taken it for granted that we had read Gibbon and Macaulay for ourselves and therefore needed no summaries or direct commentaries. Instead he was giving us the background to Gibbon and Macaulay: an analysis of the condition of history-writing before they set to work, and of the historians who influenced them. But he never spelled that out, or if he did at the very beginning of his lecture series and I missed it, he never recapitulated the point later. Lecturers should make clear what they are seeking to do. When they do not, you may have to work it out instead.

Whenever you hear a lecture that you can tell is scholarly, but whose essential point you find hard to grasp, try to work it out for yourself (and then consult your fellow students): but do not give up on the lectures.

Some lecturers – the best – give you ideas and examples you cannot yet find in print (many books and articles first began as lectures). So you need to take good notes. *Ideally your notes should give a fellow student who could not attend a clear summary of what was said.* You should not sit passively in lectures, just writing down what you hear; rather you should be thinking about it all the time, asking yourself how convincing it is, how far the evidence cited supports the conclusions, how much it tells you that is new. Your notes should also include your own comments and responses to what you heard, including aspects that would be worth going back to. In a typical lecture in the arts and social sciences, you should not attempt to take down every word. Lectures are not meant as dictations nowadays, and you would in any case find it very hard to take down everything. Pick out the main points, the best arguments, the most interesting details, the places in which a lecturer is clearly talking about his or her own research, and offering you ideas and information that you could not get elsewhere. Only if you think that a lecture is utterly brilliant, or if the arguments and reasoning are so intricate that you need every detail to follow them, is it worth trying to write the lecture down word for word. Note-taking is a difficult skill, but the more practised you are, the better you will do it. Try to persuade some of your fellow students to show you their notes and see whether you can learn from each other. Ask your fellow students what they thought of the lecture afterwards. If you end up debating it, so much the better. Some lectures may not be as informative as others, but it is nonetheless good discipline always to take notes, since it forces you to pay attention. (If you are sceptical about this, try an experiment: take no notes as you listen to a lecture, and then see how much you can set down from memory afterwards.) Try to make your notes legible and clearly organised as you set them down. It is a great waste of time to have to make a fair copy afterwards. For most students it is similarly a waste of time to record lectures on tape and listen to them again slowly at leisure: only the very best lectures would deserve such respect. If you are returning to study after years away, and you are uncertain about your note-taking skills, then you may find it useful to be able to listen to a lecture twice. But do make yourself take notes during the lecture itself, and use the recording as a supplement – and try, by analysing what you realise when listening to the tape that you had missed or not fully understood, to learn to do without. Of course, if you are dyslexic, or have particular difficulties in writing fast, then recording lectures is a sensible way of proceeding. It would be worth discussing that and any other ways of meeting your needs with your personal tutor. In science subjects, it may be more important to take down everything or as much as you can. If you are worried about your technique of note-taking, do not be shy about asking your lecturer for help: ask if he or she would be willing to look at the notes that you took of the last lecture, and advise you (it would no doubt also be very interesting for the lecturer to see how far his or her lecture was taken in). And do not simply file your lecture notes away: read through them later in the day, and the next day, and before the next lecture on the course: that will not take very long, but it will be surprisingly helpful.

A contentious issue is that of handouts. Should lecturers give students handouts that summarise the content of their lectures? Departments can be criticised in the Teaching Quality Assessments if lecturers fail to provide plans of lecture content. Students often ask for them. But summaries of lectures are in the end unhelpful. A summary you have made for yourself, while listening intently and thinking carefully about what the lecturer is saying, is much more valuable, simply because it is your own creation. You have made the content of the lecture your own – you have 'internalised' it, to use the jargon. If you simply pick up the lecture handout and file it with all the others, you have not 'internalised' it – its contents lie inert in your file. And it is precisely because the making of notes at lectures is indeed a demanding intellectual exercise, fostering and testing many different skills, that it is worth doing.

Another issue is whether a lecture should be straightforwardly delivered by a lecturer, or whether the lecturer should break it up into sections, asking for questions, or setting some exercises, for example getting students to answer questions on the handouts. The problem with such methods is that they reduce what the lecturer can get through, and if the point of a lecture is to hear the lecturer's ideas, then that does not seem sensible. On the other hand, if what the lecturer wishes to do is to convey some basic information or techniques, then such styles of teaching may work better.

Turn up on time. But if you are unavoidably late, do go in even if you have missed some minutes. Slip in as quietly as you can, but if there is no alternative but to go to the front being noticed by everyone, just do it, without looking around, as if it was quite natural. And after the lecture, go to the lecturer and apologise (don't explain, just apologise).

In most universities there are lectures by visiting speakers, special lectures (to be asked to give them is seen as a great honour), and seminars at which papers are given by graduate students working for their PhDs, your lecturers and visiting speakers. Obviously these are pitched at something more than first-year student level. But such lectures and seminars can be very stimulating, even if some parts are too advanced for you, or if the topics are not of immediate and direct relevance to your studies. At some universities there are student subject societies that organise talks by visiting speakers – get involved and invite anyone whose books and articles have made an impression on you.

Chapter 10

Classes, seminars and tutorials

In 'redbrick' universities teaching was initially predominantly by lecture, as it is in most continental universities still. But in the 1960s there was a significant shift leading to the general extension of regular meetings of groups of students, sometimes as few as four, sometimes a dozen or a score, chaired by the lecturer, but in which the emphasis would be on discussion. Such meetings are confusingly called classes and tutorials (especially if the numbers are small) or seminars (if the numbers are larger) (but I shall use these words interchangeably).

One or two students are asked to start the class going, perhaps by reading out their essays or making formal presentations, or, more often nowadays, by offering a short report. One or two other members of the group are sometimes required to respond. If it works, classes of this kind can be very useful. But there are many potential problems.

Classes depend on the interaction between teacher and student, and between students. But what happens when the students have not done enough preparation to make such discussion worthwhile? Your tutor would ideally wish to discuss with you the most difficult and complex aspects of the set topic, but if you have not got to grips with the basic facts, you are not yet ready to take part in serious discussion. This is the main drawback to class-based teaching.

If all you have done is listen to the lecturer's lecture on the topic, then that is unlikely to be enough. You need to read widely, and to think about what you have read, in the same way that you would when preparing an essay. You are then in a position to take part in a serious discussion. If you have not done any personal reading on the topic, you are not. Imagine that you have a class that is to discuss Thomas More's *Utopia*. If you have not read and reflected on the book, then you will not be able to contribute very much. If you are shameless, you may be bold enough to ask questions. Who was Thomas More? What does the word

'Utopia' mean? What exactly are More's ideas? But these are very basic questions which it would have been much better for you to have asked and begun to answer yourself beforehand by reading the book. And if the tutor or some of the other students offer you answers, that may be helpful to you, but much of it will be low-level stuff, and because you have not read *Utopia* yourself, you will have no way of telling whether what you are being told is true or important. A class in which the students are mostly not well-informed cannot be very productive. Sadly, nothing comes of nothing.

The danger then is that classes turn into private debates between the teacher and one or two other students who have done enough preparation, or into unplanned mini-lectures by the teacher. That is not altogether a waste of time, since you can learn something even from listening to a dialogue between the lecturer and the well-informed student, and because the lecturer's unplanned mini-lectures might actually be more effective than the more formal lectures, since the teacher will not be straining to squeeze in a great deal of information. But overall it is not very satisfactory if most of the class sit there like dummies.

Tutors often try to stimulate participation by asking questions, often a series of questions each slightly modifying or extending the one before, trying to draw out what you already know, or at least know in part or in general terms, so that you can be shown how to build on it. When a tutor asks a question in class, he or she is not testing you, is not wanting to show up your ignorance or incomplete understanding, and by contrast demonstrate his or her own learning. Rather the tutor wants to show you how to develop your learning. The tutor suspects that you have some idea about the topic, but perhaps only a hazy or incomplete one. So asking a question, getting a response, then asking another question that builds on that response, prompting a further response, and then another question, can be very valuable in showing you how to explore, what more you could find out to add to what you already know, how to make connections, how to ask whether a claim rests on sound evidence or not. Tutors who ask questions in this way usually have a rough idea of the points they want discussed, and their questions are intended as a means of guiding you towards them. When tutors in class ask questions, it is also a way of stopping the class turning into a monologue by the tutor. So respond to the tutor's questions.

Obviously some lecturers are more effective at stimulating a class than others; some are better with certain sorts of students. Once again that is largely a matter of personality and there is little that can be done to change that. If your tutor asks impossibly difficult questions, responds sarcastically, or ignores your answers, then that is manifestly wrong. But my impression is that most university teaching is not like that. Much more likely when you have that sort of impression is that your tutor finds it difficult to put himself in your shoes and is expecting too much of you – perhaps unreasonably, perhaps justifiably (how much preparation have you done?). Try to help. If you are asked something very difficult, say so, and counter by asking if it could be explained further; admit your ignorance but ask where you could best find out and how; if you have offered some suggestions and they have not been built upon by the tutor, repeat them and ask whether you could not return to them.

What can you do to make classes work? You can try to do sufficient work to make each class worthwhile. (That will mean doing a great deal more reading than is required just for the assessed essays you are asked to write.) At least you will then benefit. But there is not much you can do if your fellow students do not work as hard, and you will feel frustrated by their limited contributions. And, depending on the structure of the degree course as a whole, you may be taking too many different courses at once to be able to prepare as thoroughly as this for a seminar in each of your courses every week.

At the very least, you can do the specific tasks that you are set. If it is your turn to start things going, present as clear and as brief a report as you can, and remember that most of your fellow students will need very basic guidance. Include questions that open the subject out for further discussion. If there are matters of controversy, draw attention to them. The way you present your paper or report will reflect your character in the same way as I have suggested above that lecturers' personalities are reflected in their lecturing styles: it may be difficult to do very much about it. If you are very softly spoken, try to speak more loudly. However shy you feel, try to look at your audience from time to time: lift your eyes from what you are reading (put your finger on the word you have just reached so that you will easily find it again when you turn back to your text): that will keep your fellow students attentive. Try to vary the speed at which you are reading or speaking. Emphasise your main points. When the tutor opens the class to discussion, be ready to ask further questions, especially if the discussion is sticky. Whenever I give a lecture or paper after which questions are asked, I always have something in reserve in case there are not many ('Another interesting point which I did not have time to include in my talk is …').

Some lecturers more or less force every member of a class to speak, though that can be difficult when groups are ten or 15 or more, while other lecturers, realising that some students are shy or have not done all that much work, do not wish to embarrass them in front of their fellow students and are ready to allow them to remain silent. If you have not done any preparation, it is not much fun being made to speak: the best thing is to come ready at least to ask some general questions, perhaps relating the topic under discussion to one that you have previously prepared for; nor is it much fun to sit silently through a class in which no one has anything very profound to say, just rather simple and basic remarks, with no sense of direction, and where the tutor's mini-lecture is not very interesting.

Do not be afraid to speak out in a class, especially when you have done some preparation, or if you have a question to ask. But do not think that you need to have a stunning point of unparalleled originality to make before you can speak. And if it does go wrong, and your lecturer or a fellow student pounces on you, do not be downhearted. You will never make the same mistake again! Keep on trying. A good technique is to ask your teacher directly what he or she thinks of X's article on the reading list arguing such-and-such. Look at the latest issues of the journals in your subject: if there is an article on the topics being treated on your course, ask the tutor what he or she thinks of it, and whether it would help you to read it.

Even if you are too shy to speak, and are firmly resolved not to, at least practise in your own mind. When the tutor asks a question, do not just sit there waiting. Think what could be said and at least say it to yourself silently. When a fellow student says something, force yourself to summarise to yourself in your own words what has been said, and silently practise a response. This is not as helpful as actually speaking out in the class, but it will ensure that you remain alert, that you will take away some benefit from the class, and, who knows, perhaps you will before long feel confident enough to contribute.

But do not speak just for the sake of speaking, watch out if you find yourself speaking a great deal, especially if you know that you have not done any preparation. Ignorant know-alls can be very irritating in classes, especially if tutors are too polite to stop them.

Classes can be used for more than just discussions of that week's topic. They are the best place to raise questions arising from the previous week's lecture. If something has puzzled you, or has been controversial, ask your tutor if you can raise it in class. Come prepared to ask. If you have been reading – perhaps preparing for an essay – and come across something you do not fully understand, tell your class. 'Could I raise one thing that's been puzzling me, even though it's not really connected to this week's topic ...', you could say, and, especially if the class has not been sparkling, your question will very likely be welcomed.

University teachers are engaged in research and are contributing to knowledge and understanding of the subjects they teach, as I emphasised in Chapter 2. That will be true of those who are taking your classes. Find out what their precise research interests are. Look up in the library and on departmental webpages what books and articles they have written, and read them. Tell your lecturers what you thought of them! Ask your lecturers, perhaps in those awkward minutes when the class is waiting for latecomers, what book or paper they are currently working on. That would be genuinely enlightening, and if the alternative is a desultory class with broken discussion, it might be much more interesting to listen to your lecturer's latest thoughts and discoveries.

Do take notes in class. Some students only take notes in lectures, but points made in classes can be just as valuable. And include in your notes questions that the tutor asked and you could not answer, or could answer only very generally, and then do some work on them later.

Do not miss classes. These are usually compulsory. If it is your task to make a presentation or start things off, it is discourteous to your fellow students if you cut the class. Get to the class on time. If you are late, come as soon as you can, and apologise quickly – do not explain – when you come in. At the end of the class apologise again to the tutor. Of course, if you are ill, then your priority is getting better, so do not worry about missing the class. Do not struggle in sneezing and coughing over the group. Telephone or e-mail in advance, tell the departmental secretary, or ask a friend to bring a message.

Tutorials

If you are lucky, if you are at Oxford or Cambridge or a few other universities, you will regularly be taught in tutorials (Oxford) or supervisions (Cambridge) in which there will be your tutor and just you, or just you and one other student, and you will go to such tutorials with the same tutor weekly for the whole term. You will have to do rather more work than your friends in other universities: you will have to do an essay a week or even three a fortnight. And in the tutorial your tutor will offer you constructive criticism, guiding you to do better. In such a tutorial your tutor may quite deliberately try to tear your essay to pieces, challenging everything you have argued, calling on you to produce evidence in support of every claim you have made, and quite possibly making you feel very inadequate and inferior. But your tutor is not being maliciously destructive: he or she is trying to show you how you should be reading critically as you prepare your essay, questioning the books and articles you are reading, and moreover he or she is trying to provoke you into arguing back, into defending your points. Nothing works better in a tutorial than a cut-and-thrust debate, rather like a prolonged rally in tennis. And since you have to write an essay for next week, you have an immediate opportunity to do better, and if you do, your tutor will be quick to notice and to encourage you further.

It is not possible to teach like this with classes of ten. It is not fair for lecturers to appear, even with the best of intentions, to be criticising a student's work in public in front of fellow students. So in universities without a tutorial system, you will get the benefit of constructive criticism in writing, at the foot and in the margins of the essays you write. Many students may well feel that they would prefer that less pressured style of teaching. And, however rewarding the tutorial system is for students, it is often a burden for the tutors: teaching in this way is intellectually and emotionally draining, and undoubtedly explains why many Oxford and Cambridge tutors publish less than one might expect. Another difficulty is that such a system requires tutors to teach across a wide span of the syllabus. That can be very stimulating for them, but it is once again very demanding, and it is hard for tutors to be in command of everything they have to teach: elsewhere it is much more common for lecturers' teaching to be concentrated in the areas of their research.

Chapter 11

Computers

Most probably you are already long used to computers, even if only for computer games. Increasingly computers are being routinely used in school. If your university course requires sophisticated computing techniques, you will undoubtedly be given full guidance by your tutors, and most probably you will have already made a start in your A-level studies. In the humanities and social sciences, such computing skills as you need can readily be acquired. If you are not familiar with computers, perhaps because you are a mature student, then it is well worth acquiring basic computing skills. There is not really a great deal to it – and the most frustrating things are often the most elementary (such as switching the computer on and off: to switch my computer off, I first have to click on an icon misleadingly labelled 'Start'). Universities typically offer basic courses in wordprocessing (enabling you to take notes and to write essays on a computer), on using e-mail (sending and receiving letters electronically), on searching the Internet, and using and creating databases. The awkward point about such courses is that, unavoidably, you are told too much too quickly: for the experts, using computers is so much second nature that they sometimes forget what it is like to be a beginner. Often the best way to learn to use computers is to teach yourself but to ask for specific help whenever you need it (and university computing services are usually very willing troubleshooters). If you can afford it, buy your own laptop computer so that you can use it in libraries, in your room and in the vacations at home.

A great deal of nonsense is written about computers, information technology, global communications. Ignore it. Computers are no more than a tool of learning.

Some talk in grandiose futuristic terms of students studying from home and taking whole degree courses exclusively over the Internet. My guess is that this happens, and will happen, only in the most narrowly vocational courses in which students have to master set bodies of information or techniques and in which it is useful to have repeated test-questions with the computer prompt saying 'go back and try again'. But courses like that rarely set out to foster a critical intelligence. In subjects that do, personal contact, interaction with tutor and with fellow students, is essential. You are not simply learning lots of factual information: you are reacting to it, responding to the interpretations of others, discussing your studies with your fellow students, and you will consequently benefit from the monitoring, criticism and encouragement, directly related to your work, of your lecturer/tutor. None of that can be reduced very helpfully to pre-packaged question-and-answer sessions on the computer. Just as the book did not replace the lecture, the cinema did not kill the theatre, television did not kill the cinema, the record and then the compact disk did not kill the concert, so the Internet will not replace the university. Processes yield to better processes – hot-metal presses have been replaced by computer type-setting, refrigerators have made icehouses redundant – but cultural activities, and in its broadest sense that is what university learning involves, endure because they are worthwhile in themselves. I doubt that many students would rather have stayed at home with their computers.

Computers are unlikely to replace books and journals as the basis of your studies. Books are much more practical, much easier to use. (Perhaps such a view reflects my age and experience. Wordprocessors arrived when I was in my mid-thirties: if, by contrast, you have used computers as long as you can remember, then you will probably use them more easily and routinely than older people do. But I still doubt that, given the choice, you would prefer to read a novel, for example, on the computer screen, rather than as a book.) The Internet has many useful features, of course, and it will be interesting to see just how it develops. Explore it and see. But even when it offers something, it is difficult to treat it as qualitatively different from existing means of communication. Journals, for example, are going on-line. If you want to read an article, you can in theory do so on a computer anywhere in the world. In practice it is not quite so straightforward. You need the computer, you may have to pay for access to the website, technical hitches are not infrequent, and you may not enjoy the experience of staring at a flickering screen. Even if you do, and if all works, you have got exactly what you would have got if you had found a copy of the article in the library or bought a copy of the journal in which it appears. And you still have to read the article and think about it. No computer will do that for you.

The Internet undoubtedly makes it easier to cheat. There are various sites on the web which include essay-banks from which you can download model essays and pass them off as your own. Do not do this. You risk getting caught. You might get away with it, but lecturers are increasingly knowledgeable about such sites, and new software packages may also help detection. Your fellow students may well be aware of what you are doing and report you. And if you are caught deliberately and regularly plagiarising, the consequences can be devastating. More importantly still, if you cheat, you are not learning, and you are not developing your mental powers. There is no substitute for reading and thinking and working out your own ideas. Treat the Internet as another place from which you can learn – but do not cheat.

The advantage of the Internet is that its storage capacity is so vast and that, with the right software, it is very easy to create one's own webpages. That means that there is an increasing amount of material quickly and easily available to everyone. For example, I now put the reading lists I give my students on the Web: anyone interested can make use of them too. Many university teachers are doing the same. If you want to find such information, using one of the search engines on the Web (Google is generally acknowledged to be the best) can quickly give you a great deal of basic information. It can sometimes do even better than that. University teachers are beginning to put unpublished papers, lectures and talks on their webpages. For keen students, that can be a good way of keeping ahead of the game.

But remember that anyone can put anything on a website on the Internet. There is no quality control at all. How can you be sure that you are not downloading rubbish? By contrast books and especially articles in learned journals go through a lengthy process of vetting before they are accepted and published. So using the Internet means that you have to be more alert, more critical, than ever.

Chapter 12

Preparing and writing essays and assignments

Preparing an essay

When you have an essay to write, think about the general topic, and about the precise question set, before you start reading. Look at the precise wording of the question, and pick out key words and key concepts. Try to define them and then look them up in a dictionary. Jot down some preliminary thoughts and questions. That will help you to engage with the books and articles you are reading.

Select carefully what you are going to read. Look at what your lecturer has recommended, and make sure you read what is the most important. When you have an assignment to prepare, don't just wander up and down the corridors of the library, looking at what is on the shelves. Not every book is as good as every other book, and some are so important that you cannot afford to ignore them. Of course, there may be practical problems in getting hold of books and journals when you want them, especially in the less well-funded universities, but in the end you will just have to get hold of them. Perhaps you have friends at other universities who can help. Budget so that from time to time you can afford to buy a book that is not to be found in the library at the time you need it (maybe you could persuade some of your fellow students on the course to club together and buy it jointly). If your lecturer has strongly recommended a book, then do use it, even if you do not like it (though do tell your tutor why). In some subjects the lecturer may recommend a book entitled 'First Year Economics' or 'Second Year Physics' which will become your Bible: you will be expected to read it line by line, chapter by chapter, week by week. (*Buy* books of that kind.) But in a subject such as history it is important to get to know a wide range of views, so you must look at a wide range of books and articles: there will be no 'Bibles'.

The reading lists that you will get at university are often enormous. That is not because we are showing off how much we have read or want to intimidate you, but rather because we want to give you a list of all the worthwhile books and articles on a topic – and we know that the most committed students do read a great many of them, as we ourselves did as students. Do not feel intimidated. Sometimes it may seem that there is just too much to read for any human being to cope with it – but do not be daunted. Make a list of what you would ideally read, determine what is immediately relevant to your needs, and what only broadly relevant, mark what looks particularly good (perhaps because it is written by someone whose earlier writings you enjoyed), mark what your lecturer has especially recommended, but then make a start on one of the important books, without worrying about the others.

There are different types of writing. In my subject, history, there are introductory textbooks that offer a survey and summary of the field. Use them as basic guides, especially if the period of history you are studying is unfamiliar to you, but remember that such books are summaries. When they are recent, they will (if they are good) usefully pull together the latest work of others, but, as you can see, they do not go on fulfilling this function for long. Look at the date that a textbook was first published: look at its bibliography, and especially at the dates of publication of the books and articles cited there – what is the most recent? If you are now reading a textbook published in 1971 and citing books published no later than 1969, you can grasp its limitations: if you read this textbook, then you will learn nothing based on anything published after it was written – and that was quite a long time ago. To be fair, when textbooks are written by very intelligent historians, then they can be very stimulating, and remain so long after they were first published. But most textbooks are not as good as that, and it is most commonly the case that the good general book promises more than it delivers. Moreover, if you only read textbooks, then you will only be able to repeat them. Textbooks rarely contain sufficient detail for you to make up your own mind about an issue. That is where monographs and articles score.

What the good student in history will read is monographs and articles in historical journals. These are the fruit of the research of historians as described in Chapter 2 above. Here historians have the space to go into their subjects in depth and in detail, working out their ideas, offering evidence in support, and dealing with different views. Because monographs and articles are so detailed, they offer the attentive reader the opportunity to judge the arguments they put forward. The writer takes you through the sources and explains his or her own reasoning. Sometimes you will be persuaded; sometimes you may think that the evidence put forward actually points to a different conclusion. History is full of debate, and the good student will compare and contrast what different historians have said on the same issues.

In reading monographs and articles, you have to be sensible. Your lecturers should give you advice on which books and articles are the most significant. Quite often a monograph can go into great technical detail on a fairly narrow topic, and it may not be worth your time to read it all very carefully: but it may be very worthwhile to read parts of it slowly while skimming the rest, trying to extract from it the central arguments and the principal evidence in support, looking at the intro-duction and the conclusion, and at the ends of individual chapters, rather than worrying about every detail.

It is worth practising getting a sense of what a book is about very quickly. I frequently go to bookshops such as Blackwells in Oxford that have tables on which recently published books are displayed. If a title catches my eye, then I browse through the book: reading the dust-jacket blurb, the author's preface, the table of contents, and – more skippingly – the introduction, the conclusion, and, using the index, perhaps the treatment of a particular point. In a few minutes I have formed a rough impression of what the book is about and how the author is treating the subject. This is a technique well worth exploring with all the more sub-stantial books that you will encounter. Of course, it is easier for me since I am already familiar with the field and I can no doubt make sense of a new book on Tudor history more readily than I might have done as a student. And it is not enough to do this and no more. If you never read any monograph in full, you will be missing out on the most important work that historians do. But this is a useful way of deciding which books deserve to be given greater attention. If I find myself getting more and more interested as I browse through a new book in a bookshop, then I make a mental note that this is a book to be read properly. If I can afford it, I often buy it there and then; if not, I resolve to get the library copy.

Articles in historical journals are usually monographic in form; that is, they are based on deep research on particular topics, but because they are shorter they are more manageable as reading. They are more difficult to skim, but very often the introductory paragraphs are a very useful summary of the state of knowledge before the writer set to work and the concluding paragraphs usually summarise the claims of the article. Some journals require authors to give abstracts. Quickly grasping the basic point of an article by looking at introductions, conclusions and abstracts is very sensible; it again becomes easier when you already have some grounding. Of course, skimming like this does not enable you fully to understand how and why the writer has reached the conclusions that are offered: to do that you would have to read the article carefully.

Read book reviews. In history it is standard for the leading journals, the *Times Literary Supplement* and even the broadsheet newspapers to publish reviews of books. These reviews, usually between 500 and 2000 words long, are very useful as a short-cut for hard-pressed students. They will offer you a summary of the main arguments in a book. But reviewers do not just pick up the most important points. They relate the book to its subject: they may summarise the state of knowledge beforehand and what the book has added to our understanding. And often reviewers offer criticisms of the arguments in a book. That makes them especially worthwhile when you have already read the book and formed your own impressions. It is also stimulating to read several reviews of the same book, and to think about the different points made. Reading book reviews ought to be a central part of the work of students of any subject in which the reading of books bulks large.

Valuable too are review articles in which the reviewer deals with several recent books or the more general state of play in a branch of the subject. Once again these can be invaluable quick ways of getting to grips with what has been going on, while being especially stimulating if you have already read many of the works under discussion.

If you are studying literature, make your first priority the works of literature on your syllabus. Read *Hamlet* or *Paradise Lost* before you read any critics: and do not be afraid to read your texts more than once. Form your own impressions. Only then look at commentaries, and give special attention to those areas in which critics disagree with you and discuss aspects which you have overlooked, going back to the texts in order to decide whether you were right first time or not. Do not – emphatically do not – just read 'cribs', short books that appear to do all the work for you. You will be caught out, especially in the examination. Much more useful would be to read more works by the authors you are studying. If you are studying a Dickens novel, why not read one or two more, and make comparisons?

If you are studying mathematics, the sciences, engineering or medicine, you will almost certainly need to work through your principal textbook very carefully, page by page, line by line, especially complex algebra, diagrams and charts, supplementing it with intensive study of particular points, for example articles writing up the results of an experiment. You may need to grasp one point before you can go on to grasp the next point because they are so closely linked. Skimming is not much good here. In these subjects, the precise guidance of your lecturers on what to read is important and invaluable.

Read attentively (whether you are skimming or reading every word). If your mind wanders, bring it back to the matter at hand: do not day-dream, save it for later (write it down quickly if it seems a very interesting dream). Do not get up and look at the paper or the television or the Internet or make a cup of coffee. With luck, either the book you are reading will be so interesting that you will be totally absorbed by it, or you will have got so gripped by the subject that you will be devouring whatever you can find to read about it. But if neither is the case, you will have to make an effort. Remember how hard sportsmen train before an event: what you are doing is the equivalent. The ideal is total con-centration. An hour of that is worth several hours of broken attention.

Read critically. *Constantly question what you are reading.* Are the facts correct (as far as you can judge)? Is the writer making a good case? Is the evidence put forward to back up points compelling? Does one step in the argument logically lead to the next? Such questioning should be constructive, not destructive: the point of doing this is not to make the book or article you are reading seem worthless, but rather to grasp what exactly a writer's case rests on, and to strengthen and to refine it. The more you read and the more you know, the more readily and the more effectively you will be able to do this.

Some things are best read more than once. That is obviously true of lit-erary texts, since they rarely yield up everything on first reading. Expect to read the texts of such works several times. If you are studying a sub-ject for which a large introductory book is recommended as your 'Bible', then expect to read chapters again and again. In subjects such as history, it is more useful to be aware of a large range of writing, but here it can be valuable to re-read particularly important or controversial works, at least in part. If you read an article by one scholar and then another attacking it, there is much to be said for re-reading the first, and then trying to read those parts on the same aspects together. That will help you to make up your own mind.

Be aware that many topics are the arena of fierce argument and bitter controversies. You must be aware of them. To refer to an example of my own work again, it is not enough for you to have read my article on the fall of Anne Boleyn arguing that she was guilty of adultery. You will be expected to be aware that there are many historians who have argued that she was innocent, and to offer your own reasons for agreeing with me – or with them. If you just offer one side of an argument, and espe-cially if you do not seem to realise that there is more than one side, then you will not impress your lecturer, not least if he or she has been an active participant in the debates.

Always takes notes when you read or (if it is your own book) at least mark important passages in the margin or underline the text. Taking notes helps you to concentrate, forces you to think about what the author is saying, and helps imprint in your memory what you have been reading. Try to take notes economically. Use abbreviations such as C19 for 'nineteenth century', or for names or countries. Do not make full transcripts but summarise the important points in what you are reading in your own words. Formulate your thoughts in this form: 'The purpose of this book is to show that ...', 'the main points in this chapter are ...', 'the claim in this paragraph is ...'. Your notes must be summaries: there is no point in copying out whole pages word for word. Force yourself to decide what is important. Read a paragraph, read a chapter of a book, and try to summarise what it says: then read it again, and see whether you have made a fair summary. Copy out in full only really striking and memorable sentences, or sentences that encapsulate the writer's argument. Always try to summarise in your own words first. Include in your notes your own comments on what you are reading, both arguments that you find convincing or unconvincing (but note exactly why), and anything that what you are reading stimulates you to explore later. Make sure to take down the author's name, the title of the book, or the title article and the name of the journal or book in which it appears, together with page references: nothing is more frustrating than having a good quotation in your notes but being unable to say where it came from.

Writing an essay

Read carefully through the notes that you have been making on the books and articles you have been reading, and through any relevant notes you have made in lectures and classes. It is worth doing this part-way through your reading, but obviously the most important time to do it is when you have read all you are going to have time to read. Go back, too, to the jottings you made before you started your reading. Begin to organise your material under headings. Think carefully about the precise question you have been asked. Try to see patterns and trends, to find links between different aspects. Gradually plan the structure of your essay, a main interpretative line, divided up into, say, half a dozen themes that will make up your overall argument. The more you plan out an essay, the easier it will be to write. If your subject is a controversial one, pretend you are a lawyer and put down first the arguments on one side, then on the other, and then ask how each of the lawyers would respond to the other's arguments. Doing that will help you work out your own line. If not, go for a walk and imagine yourself telling a friend about the subject. Remember that in subjects such as history, there are no 'right' answers guaranteed to get you high marks. There are indeed historical facts – the Second World War broke out in 1939, Mrs Thatcher resigned as Prime Minister in 1990 – but you will not be tested on facts alone at university. What we want are *your* arguments, your interpretations. In the course of putting those forward, you will necessarily refer to facts, and show whether you have a sound factual knowledge or not, but it will not be those facts that determine your marks. What will count far more are your powers of reasoning, and the effectiveness of the way in which you draw larger arguments from the details. Completely opposite arguments can both score very high marks. Imagine your tutor asking you, 'But what do *you* think?' I wish I could give you exact instructions on how to have ideas, but how we have ideas is in the final analysis mysterious. It is not like boiling an egg, an exercise for which I could give you very precise instructions. All I can say is that when I have studied an issue, read about it, reflected on it, tried to order my thoughts, I have usually come to have things to say.

If you can, talk about your essay-in-the-making with fellow students, and also with interested friends and relatives who do not know much about your subject. Try to explain to them what your essay is about. If you can do that fluently and fully, then you can be confident that you have mastered the topic you have been set. If you cannot do that, then most probably you still need to read and to think more about the topic before you start to write the essay.

When I was a student I used to work out anything from half-a-dozen to a dozen themes, and number them. Next I would go through my notes with a different coloured pen from the one which I had used in making them, and write down the number of the theme wherever I found a point that related to it. Then I would write down each theme at the top of a sheet of paper, and go through my notes, laboriously copying out under each thematic heading all the relevant points and information I could find in my notes. Sometimes some themes would turn out to be too large, and I would sub-divide them and repeat the process, sometimes a planned theme would not work out. The next task would be to order the points and information under each thematic heading. The whole process would usually prompt further thoughts and questions, and, if time allowed, I would do some more reading, re-reading or checking. Then I would settle down to write the essay. Computers now make it possible to abbreviate that process considerably, since it is so much easier to move sections of text. Nowadays at an earlier stage I tend to sketch a framework which I then fill in from further reading, but often I also revise and reorder considerably. In the past my first draft was usually my last draft; now the computer makes it possible to go through a very large number of drafts.

As you plan and write the essay, make sure that the overall argument of your essay is closely related to the precise question set, not just vaguely to the general subject. Treat a separate theme in each paragraph. Make sure that each paragraph is logically linked to the paragraph before and the paragraph that follows. Do not refer to the same theme in four different places: group the material relating to it together in one place. Argue consistently: do not say one thing in one part of the essay and the opposite in another.

Pay attention to the introduction and conclusion. It is often sensible to write the introduction last, so that it truly announces what you are going to do. And there should be a clear connection between your introduction and conclusion – read them both together and see if there is.

Try to say exactly what you mean. Of course, if you have not really mastered your subject, if you have not read very much, if you have not thought things through, and if you have not organised your material in something like the way suggested above, then your essay is unlikely to be clearly and agreeably written. Style is above all a matter of having something to say.

Try to write elegantly. Vary the length of your sentences. Some sentences should be short. Others can be much longer, with all sorts of dependent clauses. Embellish your essay with apt quotations if you can.

Spell and write correctly. University teachers are committed to their own subjects and they find it irritating and distracting when their students make errors of spelling and syntax that ought to have been eliminated at primary school. Read your essay through before you give it in. If you use a computer, use the spellcheck facility as well. If you do not spell well, do something about it: make lists of words you commonly mis-spell, and learn the correct spellings. (If you suffer from dyslexia, submit a certificate from a specialist, and your tutors will of course make appropriate allowances.)

If you have problems with syntax – if you write sentences without main verbs, if you use commas to do the duty of full-stops and semi-colons, if you do not know when to use an apostrophe, if you are using the wrong prepositions, and especially if you have no idea what I am talking about here – then you need to acquire a book such as Michael Dummett's *Grammar and Style* (1993) and work through it.

If you have problems with vocabulary – if your tutor points out you are misusing a word – look words up in a dictionary.

If you write badly, that creates an obstacle between what you are saying and how readily your meaning is understood. It makes a poor impression. Of course, your lecturers are far more interested in your arguments, and if these are intelligent, they will to some extent overlook your linguistic failings. But you would do well to follow up conscientiously any corrections that they make on your written work.

Beware plagiarism. Copying is cheating. Do not copy out word for word pages from a book or article, from the essay-banks on the Internet, or from another student's essay, and then submit it as if it was your own work. You are aiming at obtaining a degree which certifies that *you* have reached a certain standard. If you pass off someone else's work as your own, then that certificate will not have been honestly earned. It is also risky to cheat: your lecturers may well catch you out, and, if they do, you will be heavily penalised. In fact, students rarely plagiarise with intent to deceive. Much more common is heavy dependence: sentences and paragraphs are largely, though not wholly, copied out and reproduced in an essay because the student does not really know what to do. An article seems so impressive, so learned, so clever, that the student feels all he or she can do is reproduce it. Be more confident. Try to summarise it in your own words.

Do not expect to receive any detailed or individual guidance when you are writing essays at university. Lecturers will not normally arrange to see every student to discuss every essay beforehand. Especially when essays are assessed and the marks count towards your final degree classification, there would be a risk of giving some students more favoured treatment than others, and of compromising the assessment by giving too much direct advice. Lecturers do not want to do your work for you – and remember that they are not looking for 'the answers', but rather for your own arguments supported by the evidence you have gathered.

The best way lecturers can help you to do the best you can is after you have written an essay: then they can read it carefully and make suggestions on what you could profitably work at, suggestions that will be based on an appraisal of what you have actually done. But if you just call on your tutor and say vaguely that you are stuck, it is difficult for a tutor to know what to say. You would not want them to write your essay. Be honest with yourself. Perhaps you are uneasy simply because you have been given a great deal of freedom and you do not feel certain that you are making the most of it. Perhaps you are uneasy because you know in your heart that you have not really done all that much work on the assignment – in which case do a little more. If you have been working sensibly, be confident. Even if you are uncertain, especially in your first year, when doing your first essay, just have a go. Do what you think you ought to be doing. Almost always, students who worry like this are in fact worrying unnecessarily. Remember the first year is likely to be pass/fail only, and an essay has to be pretty bad to fail. Even more reassuring ought to be my repeated experience that it is the best students who are the most self-critical. And do not apologise or offer self-justificatory excuses when you hand in your work (unless you have been ill and your work has been interrupted): just give it in.

If you really are stuck, do not hesitate to seek help from your tutors. But remember that they may not find it easy to remember who you are, especially if you are in a group of ten they see once a fortnight, and they have seen you only once. So if you call on them, say, 'Hello, I'm X', and remind them of your name and the course you are taking before you tell them about your worry. Remember also that lecturers are busy folk and that teaching you is only part of their duties. Do not expect to find them sitting in their offices waiting for you to drop by; note your tutor's office-hours; use e-mail.

Solving problems

In the sciences you are very likely to be asked to work through problems. To do that you will need to have a sound grasp of the principles involved and to go logically step by step through the problem. You will be marked not only on whether your answer is correct but on the steps of reasoning that you have used. All that is very different from the work of students in humanities and social science disciplines. But the process of logical and deductive reasoning – moving from one stage to the next in a clear sequence – is something that humanities and social science students can profitably ponder too.

In the sciences you are often asked to set out properties and qualities factually, but in great detail and precisely. Again students in the humanities and social sciences might benefit from attempting such levels of detailed precision.

In the sciences you will need to be able to produce diagrams, graphs and charts; to handle algebra; to calculate quantities and relationships – a kind of precision that is different from that in the humanities.

Studying languages

Learning a language is the easiest thing in the world, Colin Morris, one of my tutors, once assured me – before going on to say that it was also the hardest. It's easy because all you need to do is to devote half an hour every day to it. But that, he continued, is also the most difficult thing in the world. Most people find such regular and sustained commitment to something very demanding. But if you are studying a language, there is no escape from learning vocabulary, from learning the conjugations of verbs, from grappling with grammar.

Living in a country in which the language is spoken is by far the best way of mastering it. If, for example, you are planning to study French at university, try to spend a gap year or at least a long summer vacation in France beforehand, and go to France or other French-speaking countries whenever you can. When you go abroad, try to stay with a family. Watch television, listen to the radio and read newspapers. Immerse yourself in the language. Avoid meeting English speakers: try to think in the language you are studying.

There are many foreign students at British universities. Make contact and offer to help them with their English if they will help you with your chosen foreign language: meet regularly to practise conversation. It sounds rather contrived, but overcome your nervousness, and you will find the benefits.

Dissertations and longer essays

In subjects such as history in your final year you will usually be expected to write an extended essay (perhaps 5000–6000 words) or a dissertation (up to 10,000 words). Many students are somewhat daunted by the prospect of writing more than they ever have before on any topic – but most of them finish by wishing they were allowed to write more. And most find preparing a dissertation among the most rewarding things that they do as students.

You will choose a topic in consultation with your tutor. It is important to pick a topic that interests you but that is also manageable, so you should discuss it carefully with your tutor, and be prepared to adjust it in the light of what you find.

Bear in mind that extended essays, and above all dissertations, are expected to be qualitatively different from your earlier written work. Beware if you find that you are just doing the same as you did in Years 1 and 2, only at greater length: make sure that you really have grasped what is expected. Plagiarism is a particular temptation, since a dissertation appears very much like a standard academic paper. But do not think that it will be acceptable simply to take someone's article or chapter of a book and essentially reproduce it (maybe just changing the wording here and there).

What is required varies between subjects, reflecting the different characteristics of different disciplines. In history, for example, it is expected that dissertations will be based on sources, usually edited in print: the records of governments, ambassadors' despatches, legal records, chronicles and contemporary letters, newspapers and so on. You will be expected to concentrate on those sources that are relevant to your chosen topic. Of course you will also be expected to read the books and articles on it written by modern historians. But take care not to let yourself be too easily influenced by them. Be confident. Read the sources – and read them again and again. You will be expected to show that you have subjected your sources to careful criticism. Who wrote this letter? To whom was it sent? When was it written? Why was it written? Is it genuine? What is its context? Are there other sources that corroborate or contradict it?

Dissertations and extended essays based on sources must be properly referenced. If you quote or summarise details drawn from your printed sources or if you quote or summarise modern scholars, you should give a reference. The point of giving references is not to parade your scholarship but is simply so that anyone reading your work can easily verify what you say. If, for example, you quote a resident ambassador's opinion of Cardinal Wolsey, and I want to follow it up, I need to know where it can be found. If you cite the book and the page in which it appears, then I can readily track it down.

An especially fruitful technique – though a time-consuming and demanding one – is to take an article by a modern scholar on your chosen topic, and to look up the references in the footnotes one by one, as far as is practical, looking to see how the scholar has deployed the material. Sometimes you will be impressed by how intelligently the scholar has made connections, sometimes you will be astonished by blunders and misunderstandings.

Students preparing dissertations often get very worried about presentation. Of course, presentation should be as perfect as possible. But it is not the most important feature: the arguments and evidence are what really count, so do not panic. Citations should be given according to the conventions in your subject. Your lecturers will advise you and it is always best to follow their instructions (I usually tell my students not to worry if they adopt a different scheme by mistake provided that they are consistent).

Understanding the history of your subject

It is well worth while standing back from the daily and the weekly pressures from time to time, and trying to find out something about the history of the subject that you are studying. You will be busy with your immediate studies: in history, you may be reading about Henry VIII, Hitler or the Industrial Revolution; in English, you may be reading Shakespeare or Joyce; in economics you may be learning about the demand curve, and so on. But what you should try to grasp is that the subjects you are studying have themselves evolved and developed over time and it enriches your understanding of what you are studying now if you have some idea of how things came to be as they are now. A good way of getting into this kind of approach is to begin by looking at the lives of famous practitioners of your discipline: look at famous historians such as Clarendon, Gibbon, Macaulay, Trevelyan, Namier, or famous physicists such as Newton and Einstein, or economists such as Adam Smith, Ricardo and Keynes. That is the kind of enquiry that at a basic level encyclopedias or the Internet can help you with. At a more sophisticated level, look at how the subject you are studying came to be organised in the way that it is currently set out in university syllabuses. Ask your lecturers to help you with books to read and aspects to explore – something for the long summer vacations.

Thinking about the nature of your subject

It is also well worth thinking generally about the nature of knowledge in your subject. If you study philosophy, you will of course study theories of knowledge. But it is fruitful to ask such questions whatever the subject you are studying. What do we mean when we say that something is true? How would we persuade a sceptic that the claims we are making – as historians, as physicists – are true?

Extra-curricular reading

It is sometimes objected against university syllabuses that they are too specialised and too narrow, but that is unavoidable given how much there is to learn. It is much better to study something in depth, and to master it, than to pick up a smattering of this and that. The best way forward is to combine formal study of one or two subjects in depth with broad extra-curricular interests.

The best students are interested not just in the syllabuses they are studying but much more broadly. Browse the shelves of your university library from time to time (though not when you are supposed to be getting on with an essay) and dip into any book or journal, on any subject, that catches your attention. Quite possibly you may stumble across something of direct relevance to your studies (in which case be sure to take down the reference to the book). But wider reading will inform and enrich your studies in countless ways.

Read a serious broadsheet newspaper daily (*The Times, The Independent, Financial Times, The Daily Telegraph, The Guardian*) and look at some of the weeklies (*The Economist, The Spectator, Times Literary Supplement*). Whichever subject you are studying at university, you will find relevant points from time to time – book reviews, obituaries of famous scholars in the subject you are studying – but you will absorb a lot more in general.

Talk to your fellow students who are studying other subjects about what they are doing. Ask them to recommend a book they have found especially stimulating. Occasionally drop into a lecture on another subject, perhaps when some well-known visitor comes to the university. You may not follow everything but you should gain something.

Vacation study

It used to be very common for universities to expect students to spend a large part of their vacations studying. If you were at a university which required you to take major examinations, and especially final examinations, in which your degree depended on the examinations you took at the very end of your course, then it was essential to study in the vacations. At Oxford and Cambridge, six-week vacations at Christmas and Easter, and 14-week summer vacations allowed a good deal of time for such work. At Oxford it was also common for tutors to set practice examinations at the beginning of each term on the previous term's work. At other universities, the academic year has been longer (three ten-week terms in the redbrick universities, and now two 15-week semesters, of which the first 12 are for teaching), and vacations, especially at Christmas and Easter, have not really been long enough for sustained work.

Nowadays most students need to work for money in the vacations, especially in the summer vacations. Moreover the increasingly prevalent system of mini-examinations immediately after a course has been taught means that there is little direct point in doing more reading on a course if you have already been examined on it and your marks have been set down in concrete.

But when you can use vacations – maybe at Christmas and Easter – then do so. Read that big book that there was never time for in term. In a vacation whole days may be free for uninterrupted reading.

Chapter 13

Revising for examinations

The preliminary to preparation for examinations is to find out what kind of examination you face. For ease of explanation, I shall divide them into two types, 'major' and 'mini'. That is a little artificial since the differences between them are more blurred than that sharp division suggests, but it will make my point clearer. Major examinations are challenging and difficult. They require you to answer four or three questions in three hours. The questions cover all and any aspects of the syllabus, and they often touch on lesser topics or give more familiar topics an unexpected twist. The examination questions are devised and the scripts marked, completely or mostly, by examiners who have not taught you. Written examinations of this kind grew up in the nineteenth century: before that, oral tests were the standard form of assessment. It was held that written examinations of this type were a much fairer and more objective way of judging whether students had mastered a syllabus and which had done better than others. The prospect of major examinations of this kind concentrated the minds of students who knew that they had to cover the ground and who realised that anything they studied during a course might be of use in the examination.

Major examinations survive in a few universities as a general rule, especially at Oxford and Cambridge. In certain subjects, especially those which are more vocational, and in which professional bodies outside the universities lay down the syllabus and the standards required to pursue a career in those professions (medicine, engineering, law), major examinations remain the norm.

But in most universities and in most subjects, major examinations have been modified – sometimes by a clean-break reform, sometimes by the accumulation of piecemeal changes – into mini-examinations. Indeed in a few universities and subjects, examinations have been abandoned altogether. If you are terrified of examinations, but desperate to go to university, you can now find such courses. More common is a combination of continuous assessment – the essays done during the course count for a percentage of the total marks – and mini-examinations.

Mini-examinations are written examinations held under formal conditions. They are shorter than the major examinations. They last two hours, an hour-and-a-half, or just an hour. Students are required to answer just one or two questions. Sometimes these questions are broken up into shorter exercises. Mini-examinations are typically set and marked by the lecturers who have just taught the course. Do not worry about that. Scripts are now usually 'anonymised', and markers do not know whose work they are reading. External examiners vet the questions and moderate the scripts, so you can be sure that the process is fair and not biased in favour or against candidates whom the internal markers like or dislike. Since the papers are set by the teachers of the course, the questions usually reflect exactly what has been covered in the course; the questions tend to be straightforward, without much of a twist. You do not need to fear trick questions designed to catch you out. That makes them different from A levels and from major examinations. Sometimes you are allowed to take books or a file of your notes into the examination.

Why mini-examinations have replaced major examinations is a fascinating question. Since examinations are held on a set day and a set time, they were thought to penalise those who were not at their best on the day. It seemed wrong not to take into account the work that students had done during the course. The increasing numbers of mature students in higher education, many of whom had not written examination answers under pressure for years, made many teachers feel that major examinations were an unfairly severe test for them. Educational theorists elaborated a variety of ways of assessing students and argued that diversity of assessment was good in itself. Not least the vast expansion in student numbers made the reduction in the scale of examinations a contribution to survival, since it reduced the marking load. And of course students, even good and hard-working students, have frequently been nervous of examinations. However that may be, what matters to you is what kind of examination you face, since that should influence your tactics.

Revising for examinations

Calculate the number of exams you face, and the number of hours you have free, and allocate so much time per exam per day for revision. If you are taking a joint- or combined-subject degree, be sure to allow enough time for each component part, not just those you enjoy most. (In some universities you may face a mini-examination on the Monday morning after teaching for the semester has finished on the previous Friday. That is a crazy way of organising things, but if that is your lot, plan for it, and begin revision in week ten of a 12-week semester.)

Prepare a number of broad topics for examinations, beginning by extending and developing topics you have already worked up. Ask yourself what the most important topics in the course you have taken have been – those are what the examiner is most likely to set questions on.

Sometimes you can almost predict the topics that will come up in the examinations by studying examination papers over the past five or ten years. Try to set an examination paper yourself and you will quickly realise that there is only a small number of topics that it would be fair to set questions on. And there are limits to the scope for ringing the changes with questions on each topic. Study past examination papers when you can, and you should get a fairly shrewd idea of the possible questions. That should reassure you if you ever feel inclined to fret about an examination.

It is more useful to have several topics worked on in depth than it is to have covered every aspect of the syllabus superficially. That is why the essays you have already done are the best starting point for revision. Of course ideally you should have looked at everything, or at least at a great deal, but here we are concentrating on realities and tactics, and once you start revising, stop worrying about those parts of the syllabus that you have not tackled. What counts in a typical examination is the answers that you write, and even in a major examination you will not write more than three or four. If you face a major examination you will, however, need to have covered more topics than if you face a mini-examination, partly because you have to write more answers, and partly because the examiners are more likely to ask questions about lesser topics or give their questions an unusual slant. If you are revising for a mini-examination, you are much more likely to get away with regurgitating your course work, or your teacher's lecture handouts (if any), though, of course, doing that will not score high marks, and will, at best, leave you around the II:i/II:ii borderline. If you face a mini-examination, you should probably aim to work on one more topic than the number of questions you face – three topics if you will be required to write two answers – but if you face a major examination, then you would do well to think of preparing at least double the number of topics, say eight for a four-question examination and six for a three-question examination.

The essays you have written during the course, the most intensive work that you have done on it, serve as excellent aids for revision for examinations. Supplement them with the notes you have taken in lectures and in the classes you have attended. But do not think it is enough simply to leaf through these notes when the time for revision comes. And just doing that will be rather dull. What you need to do is to consolidate and to develop what you have been learning.

Keep handy a general notebook for jotting down any ideas or striking remarks or quotations relating to all your studies that occur to you – perhaps in conversation with friends, or when you read the day's papers – and references to interesting books or articles that you might read one day, even though you do not have time now.

It is a good idea to spend a little time every evening, or at least every week, during the course simply going over whatever you have been reading and whatever you have been doing in classes or hearing in lectures.

You ought to have been receiving feedback from your lecturers, above all comments on any written work you have done. Look carefully at such comments. If your lecturer suggests you need to consider aspects of a topic in greater detail or depth, or that you should look at particular points you have omitted, or that you should read some important article or additional topic that you overlooked, then you should give priority to this in your revision.

Build up a file on each of your courses. Keep your essays and other assignments in it, together with the notes you take at lectures and in classes. Work on these materials further, by building on topics you have already covered and extending them naturally, for example by linking related aspects from different essays. *Boil down your essays and your notes to a set of points*, illustrated by some details and some striking quotations, on just one or two sheets of paper per topic. There is much to be said for using bullet points, highlighting ink, subdividing points, etc. It is useful to do this well before the end of a course, especially if you face a mini-examination immediately after the end of it. If you use a notebook, leave blank pages so that you can add to your notes; or even better, use a computer so that you can perfect them at will. *Read through these boiled-down topic notes from time to time.* If you do, you will find you get to know them even though you have not actually set out to learn them by heart. And you will find that you will start making connections. Something you read or hear in a lecture will illuminate what you noted a week ago. Every so often, take a photocopy so that you can safely take them with you and, for example, browse through them on the train when you go away for a weekend.

Try to do a little new reading when revising to freshen up your notes. If an important new book or article has just appeared on one of your topics, it will be very impressive if you show that you are aware of it. Look at book reviews and at articles that offer significant reinterpretations.

Students are often nervous about examinations because they see them as tests of factual memory and they fear that their memories are poor. One reason that major examinations have been replaced by mini-examinations is that many educationalists agree with them. But there are several misperceptions here.

First, memory is a valuable and necessary skill. You are what you know, not what you can look up. In all professions and careers, you will be faced with the need to make decisions, often in a hurry, on the basis of what you know then and now.

Secondly, it is possible to train and to improve your memory, by using mnemonics and associations. A mnemonic is a sentence composed of words whose initial letters will remind you of what you want to remember. 'Richard of York gave battle in vain' will remind you of the colours of the rainbow: red, orange, yellow, green, blue, indigo, and violet. Associations can be used for remembering numbers. Think of objects that rhyme with numbers, for example:

one – gun
two – shoe
three – tree
four – door
five – hive
six – sticks
seven – heaven
eight – Tate (as in Tate Gallery)
nine – mine
ten – hen

And then turn the number you want to remember into a mental picture: the year 1536 becomes gun-hive-tree-sticks. However bizarre it may seem, it is a remarkably effective method of remembering otherwise unconnected numbers. Its origins lie in the Renaissance (see Frances Yates, *The Art of Memory*). Another way of memorising is by regular practice. Try to recall your bank account or your credit card number. Write your guess down. Look up the correct number. Try again in an hour's time. And again an hour later. And again … and again.

Thirdly, and perhaps most importantly here, whatever the benefits of a good memory, examinations are not in fact tests of memory. What counts is your power of reasoning in developing and sustaining an argument. Where memory may come in is if you know some details and facts, and particularly some striking or unusual facts, or witty remarks, and can work them into your answers. So when you are engaged in your course reading, and you come across an arresting quotation, make a special and separate note of it. Because such remarks are striking in themselves, you should remember them without trying to. Moreover the knowledge that examinations test is not recall of isolated facts of the sort that might make you a millionaire in a television quiz game, but rather more general understanding.

Do not just revise and work up topics in isolation from each other. Try to make patterns and to see connections. This is how a student can be independent and original. If you are revising for just one or two mini-examinations, then it might not be easy to see links between them. But it is still worth trying. And if you are doing major examinations, especially six or more (I faced ten), as final examinations at the end of your third year, then you should give a good deal of attention at that stage to making comparisons and contrasts between the different courses you have taken.

Try attempting practice answers without looking at any notes. Try taking a blank sheet of paper and jotting down headings, and outline answers. Look at past examination questions and make yourself attempt a few of them in full, more of them by preparing skeleton essay plans. Imagine you are giving a radio talk or being interviewed on television about the topic you are revising: what would you say? That is also a good way of practising in idle moments, say, when you are waiting at a bus stop. If after having tried to work out answers in this way you then look back at your notes, you will undoubtedly spot points that you did not think of making – and these will now stick in your mind.

If you want model examination answers, look at the leading articles in the broadsheet newspapers. They are roughly the same length, 750 words, as typical examination answers, and like examination answers they are usually written against the clock. Read them and re-read them not for the opinions advanced, but rather to analyse the way they are constructed and how the arguments are developed. See if there is anything you could usefully follow.

Your tutor should offer you a revision class devoted exclusively to revision in which you can discuss revision methods and examination techniques on the one hand, and topics that you wish to raise on the

other. Such revision classes are invaluable: do attend. But come prepared to ask questions, especially on the content of the course, and do
take notes.

Chapter 14

Examination technique

Stick to your usual routines before the examination, but do not go to a wild party the night before. Instead read through your notes and notebooks once more. Get up early and get to the examination room in good time, and keep on browsing your notebooks.

Once in the examination, look carefully through the question paper and pick out the questions that seem most promising for you. Do not spend too long on this, but settle on the best one for you.

Do spend time thinking and planning out your answer. Rushing into writing without thinking very much is risky, since the question set is unlikely to be exactly what you have prepared, and if you simply write down all you know about a topic, a good deal of your answer will be irrelevant. Quantity alone carries little weight. If people around you are writing furiously, do not be deterred, but continue planning. Before you start writing, work out your argument, so that when you put pen to paper, you know what you will say at the end of your answer. Do not be afraid to spend plenty of time on such planning. Relax and think about all the aspects of the topic that the question raises: you will be surprised how much will occur to you that can be made relevant. If you are taking an examination in which you are asked to answer two questions in two hours, spend 15 minutes thinking and 45 minutes writing your answer to each of the questions.

Divide your time up equally between each of the questions you have to answer. It is virtually impossible to do so well on two questions as to compensate for doing very badly on a third. (You can work that out for yourself: 60 per cent, 60 per cent and 0 will produce 40 per cent overall.)

Be relevant. Do not regurgitate an essay you have written before or lecture notes or handouts. Do not twist the question to fit. Almost certainly the question you will be asked will focus on a particular aspect of a topic. If you ignore this, or only make a token nod at the terms of the question at the beginning or end, then you will not get a high mark. If you are asked about an individual in the past, do not write a narrative of his or her life or career; if you are asked about some events, such as a war, do not give a recital of the sequence of events. Since you will have been asked about a specific angle, and above all to analyse why something happened, or to assess a comment made by others, you will be wasting time on offering information that is not directly relevant. Some of what you say will no doubt have some bearing on the broad subject, so you will not be in danger of failing, but you could have earned the marks by writing a fraction of your essay. Stick to the point throughout – do not wander off: that is why planning before you start writing is so useful. Do not write all you know about a topic. Stick to what the question demands.

Obviously you must show that you are in command of factual material. But do not worry, as so many students do, that you might make some blunders of fact. Do that once or twice and it will not be held against you. Only if you make so many mistakes that the examiner comes to think that you do not have a clue about the whole subject will you be in serious trouble.

Show that you are aware of different interpretations and explain why you think some are more convincing than others.

Begin boldly. Try to catch the reader's attention. Often a short and very definite opening statement can be very effective. Do not be facetious but if you can be witty, if you can say something that makes the reader smile …

Try to avoid saying the obvious; try to offer an unusual slant, especially if you are writing about a standard and popular topic. Offer your own interpretations as much as you can. Be confident to do this. Don't use 'I' but more scholarly formulations such as 'It is very likely that …', but do offer your own views. Show that you are aware that there are exceptions to what you say, but subordinate them to your main claims. Summarise your arguments in your conclusion, but if possible, do more than just summarise. Try to end with a bang, with an idea that refers back to the beginning, but with a twist.

Candidates often ask how much they can assume the examiner already knows: do they need to convey basic facts? The best way is to include such basic information economically. If you are asked 'What was the foundation of Wolsey's power?', you could begin your answer by writing 'Thomas Wolsey, the butcher's son from Ipswich who in 1515 became Lord Chancellor, Archbishop of York and a Cardinal, depended entirely on the favour of King Henry VIII'. That states the case you are going to make in your answer – that Wolsey depended on the king – but you have also dovetailed the basic facts of his career, without wasting any words. It is important to 'introduce' people you mention in essays and briefly to explain concepts, but practise doing this economically, not at length.

Do not try to invent quotations, or to bluff your way through ignorance. If you are clever enough to do this plausibly, you are clever enough to have got through by conventional means, and the risks of being caught out are considerable.

Think of yourself as an examiner, marking examination answers. Imagine what would impress you.

Enjoy examinations; enjoy the chance to show what you can do to the examiner who has no choice but to read anything you say!

Chapter 15

Feedback
How am I doing?

Unless you are reading your essays out aloud in tutorials or classes, you are unlikely these days to get any feedback quickly. Once a colleague and I challenged each other to turn round essays within 24 hours of receiving them, and we both managed it – it must have been very encouraging for students to get essays and comments back so quickly. Student numbers have risen dramatically and there are now just too many essays to be marked. And a further problem now is that essays are mostly assessed; the marks count towards the class of degree, and so in order to be fair they are all required to be given in on the same day. That means, unfortunately, that the lecturer marking them receives a huge load of essays at the same time. Some lecturers get very depressed at the mere sight of them: a recent guide to lecturers suggests that they do not leave the whole pile of unmarked essays in plain view, but hide them away under their desks, taking out only as many essays as they can mark in a single session of marking. Astonishing advice – but revealing of just how heavy the burdens and pressures on lecturers can be. It takes me anything between 30 minutes and an hour to read through an essay, usually twice, sometimes more, to correct the obvious mistakes of spelling, grammar and style, to get to grips with the structure of the essay, suggesting improvements or alternatives, and then to comment, often at length, on the content – the arguments – of the essay. Quite often I look up the books and articles which students have used, and start to ponder points made. It will take me a good while to get through that pile of essays. And the trouble is that all lecturers will be fitting in marking between taking classes, giving lectures, attending meetings, and they may well have a further batch of essays from another course. Once again the student at a financially less hard-pressed university is likely to find that the lecturers there are able to get work marked more quickly. Work that is assessed in Years 2 and 3 is further delayed because of the requirement that it be double-marked, which means that another teacher has to find the time to mark everything. Then the essays, or a selection, are sent off to the external examiner. So it can take a very long time before you learn your agreed marks. What is at fault here is the system of continuous assessment and high numbers of students to staff. If the essays were just assignments that you wrote, as preparation for an examination, but with the marks not counting, then you would not all have to give them in at the same time and lecturers would find the marking more manageably spaced out.

Feedback from examinations can also be protracted. Double-marking and moderation by external examiners takes time, and a new difficulty has been introduced by the spread of semesterisation with examinations at the end of each semester. Getting feedback to students on examinations taken at the end of semester one has been especially awkward. Lecturers may receive large batches of scripts to mark as first or as second marker just as the teaching of semester two begins; it can take several weeks before the process, including moderation by external examiners, is complete. And because universities are fearful of appeals, they often hold on to examination scripts rather than returning them to students who might well profit from the marginal comments the examiners have made.

Do not then be surprised if you submit essays and take examinations and are left for weeks, if not longer, without knowing how you have performed. It does not mean that you have done badly, just that the process of assessment is not yet complete.

The general issue is a matter that your student representatives on the departmental board should raise, though, as you can see, it is not easy to think of what can be done.

Eventually you will receive your marks. If the mark is lower than you were expecting, and if the tutor has not made it clear why, ask how you could have improved on your essay. Usually, however, tutors do comment quite fully on work. Pay careful attention to these comments on your work: reflect on them and take action as necessary. If the comments are unhelpful, or unfairly critical, do not hesitate to approach your tutor about them: send an e-mail, or go to see the tutor, always bringing the essay with you, and explain what you set out to do and why you think it meets what was required. But remember that accepting criticism of your work is an important step in doing better: do not feel angry or humiliated, but see rather how you can learn from it. Resilience in the face of difficulties is an admirable quality. Most students are above all interested in their marks, and if the marks are high enough, then they do not always bother much with the tutor's comments, but just put the essay in their file. That is a pity, because the comments and suggestions deserve very close attention. It may be too late to improve marks on that particular course, but there may be some general lessons to be learned that could be applied in your current and future courses.

You will have only a very hazy idea of how well you are doing until well after halfway in a semester-long course, and even then quite possibly not much. And you may not know how you fared altogether until well after halfway through the next semester.

Do not worry. You are most unlikely to fail Year 1. Year 1 is usually a qualifying pass/fail year, and if you have half-decent A levels then you should have no trouble passing. Very few students fail – and most of those have serious problems from the start, for example, failing to give work in at all.

And do not worry all the time how you are doing. This is something more characteristic of mature students, who are by definition embarking on what is quite an adventure, and often feel in need of reassurance that all is going well. Remember that if you are in trouble, your tutor will – eventually – tell you. But only a very few students get into real difficulties. If you feel anxious, stop worrying about how you are doing, and concentrate on the substance of the next assignment you have been set. Do not fret about the mark you will get, but concentrate on the arguments you will put forward, the evidence you have found to back them up. Whenever you find yourself worrying, say to yourself that you will postpone the worrying until after you have seen your mark for that assignment. Very likely, the mark will be fine and your worries will be shown to be exaggerated. But if you are seriously anxious about how things are going, then do ask your tutors (catch them before or after a class or lecture, e-mail them, or send a note). If you have not yet produced an assignment for them, it will of course be difficult for them to say anything informed about your progress. Once you have had work marked and been reassured – almost always you will be – then stop worrying about how you are doing in general, and get on with the next task, or with revising.

By the beginning of Year 3 you ought to know exactly how you did in Year 2, and what the chances of a first or a II:i are. Discuss your overall performance with your personal tutor at the beginning of Year 3. If some of your Year 2 marks, now that you know them, were not as good as you hoped for, go back to the lecturers on those courses, and discuss your work with them. Compare your feedback with that of your friends on the course if you can.

Conclusion
Study skills?

Of course all these tips (however much thought I have put into them) are easy for me to give you: it is much harder for you to follow them. And if you have been reading attentively, you may have noticed that for all the tips I have been offering, there is often a gap at crucial points between what I have been suggesting, and what you have to do. It is easy for me to tell you to organise your time, to plan your studies, to concentrate when you are studying, to work longer hours, to make good notes, to plan your essays, to put forward, lucidly and elegantly, your own ideas ... but exhortation does not show you *how* you can do this. I have described approaches and methods but at every point there is a crunch at which all depends on you. I could show you what I think is an excellent set of notes and urge you to do the same; but even having a model does not make it simple to follow it. The root of the matter is that the tasks you have to do, such as taking notes or working out your own ideas or writing essays or organising your time, are complex matters that cannot be reduced to a simple formula, a single set of golden rules, that everyone can easily follow. They are more of an art or a craft in which native talent combines with repeated practice to make perfect.

When I began writing this part of the book I originally headed it quite correctly 'Tips on how to make the most of your studies'. But what I told friends I was writing was a guide to the 'study skills' that university students need. That, I have come to realise in writing these chapters, is a misconception. If you look back over them, you will see that what I have been doing is rather describing the ways in which good and successful students usually study. But it is more difficult to establish cause and effect: are successful students successful because they take good notes, or do they take good notes because they are good students? Most of the tips I have offered you have been more to do with the form than the content of your study. I have urged you to take notes, or to keep a general notebook to jot down anything relevant that you come across, but I have not shown you how to do this in a way that would infallibly guarantee success. No one can tell you how to find your own ideas and arguments. I can try to describe how I worked out interpretations of my own, but even then I have had to admit that I do not quite know how I came to have the ideas that I have developed in my historical writings. There is something magical in the end about all human creativity, and, however inadequate the result may be, all student essays are an attempt at creation.

Does that mean that there are no 'study skills' that can be taught and learned? Undoubtedly, studying a rigorous subject at university does foster mental qualities which can be called skills, as I argued in Chapter 4. But these are skills learned through studying, rather than skills learned in advance or in isolation, and then brought to bear on your studies. The best way of developing those qualities is quite simply by studying a demanding intellectual discipline under the guidance of tutors who offer constructive criticism.

What place is there then for 'study skills' courses? It is becoming increasingly fashionable for university departments to put on some sort of course on 'study skills' for first-year students. If your department does offer such courses, then whatever you think of them, you should take part. If you find them bewildering, or if you find them patronisingly obvious, endure them patiently. They are not the heart of your university education. If you are fortunate, such courses will take the form of general advice in small groups from experienced teachers of your subject. Take the opportunity to raise any aspects of studying that you have found bothersome in the past. Look through this book and ask your tutor about the advice given here: is it appropriate in your subject and your department? Ask your tutor how he or she sets about studying: which methods, which habits?

More problematic are more structured initial courses on 'study skills'. New students who are less committed may well find such a course overwhelming: too many different things involved to leave any lasting impression. Moreover, if such courses involve tasks and assessments designed to foster particular kinds of skills, they risk becoming damaging. The best way to improve and develop your ability to prepare and write an essay, for example, is to do just that, and then to receive comments from your tutor. There is little point in listing all the intellectual skills, of varying degrees of difficulty, involved in preparing and writing essays, and then carrying out practice exercises in each of them separately – for example, finding books in the library, reading skills, note-taking skills, essay-planning skills and so on – and having them assessed by your tutor. 'Evidence for the effectiveness of study skill courses is extremely thin on the ground' (G. Gibbs, *Teaching Students to Learn*, Open University Press, 1981, p. 69). The trouble is that in order to write an essay you need to deploy and to combine all these skills: the whole is greater than the sum of its parts. And if you write an essay, that will test and develop all those contributory skills well enough, as well as testing and developing your powers of integration. It is a more appropriate as well as a more economical exercise. And there are no sets of rules that you can be told to follow and that, once followed, would guarantee you success.

Does that suspicion of 'study skills' courses also invalidate this book? Am I a snake-oil salesman, on my own admission promising what no one can deliver? Are my tips for students no better than the tips you can buy from 'investment advisers' for the 3.30 at Newmarket?

The first response I should make is that much of this book has been attempting something else. It is, I should claim, valuable for students to be aware of the history of universities and the commitment to research of those who teach them there. Prospective applicants would be well advised to consider the funding of universities before choosing where to apply. And all students should ponder both the ideals to which universities aspire and the realities of modern student life.

It is only in the latter part of this book that I have offered advice on how to study. Much of what I say is obvious – though not necessarily obvious to every student. Some of the points have occurred to me long after I was an undergraduate, but it would have been useful if I had grasped them at the time. For example, I was uncertain just how much of the massive reading lists I was expected to read, and none of the tutors whom I asked gave me more than an embarrassedly non-committal response. Now I should tell a student who asked how much to read, 'enough so that you feel you have mastered the subject', and define 'mastering the subject' as being able to explain it fluently and fully to others. Of course, that is exactly what I was doing, as I prepared and wrote my essays, but I was like Molière's Monsieur Jourdain, speaking prose without realising it. Much of my advice will help you realise what you are setting out to do and what is expected of you. Much of it is intended to reassure you, to offer you confirmation that you are on the right lines, that your approach is entirely appropriate. It is also intended to make you think about what you are doing, in the belief that you yourself will see beneficial additions or adjustments to your ways of working. Much of what you have been reading sets down what over the years I have been telling my students; and my impression has been that they have found it worthwhile. But its utility has not been that of a detergent that dissolves away a stain, or a wonder-fertiliser that swiftly makes a plant shoot up several feet, but rather that it conveys to them my experiences and reflections after many years of studying and teaching. There are undoubtedly skills involved in painting or in carpentry, but they cannot fruitfully be taught in abstraction. What you can do is to practice – to paint a picture or to make a chair – again and again and again. And someone more experienced than you can comment and offer specific suggestions on what you are doing which can be very useful. But in the end – and especially when what you are engaged in is an act of creativity – what matters is what you bring to it. Thus it is, I should claim, in the art of learning. I can offer suggestions drawing on my own experience but in the end what really matters is what you do yourself. Good luck!

Further reading

Two detailed tomes are indispensable when you start applying to university. Brian Heap, *Choosing Your Degree Course and University* (Trotman, 8th edition, 2002) offers brief notes on all courses. Brian Heap, *Degree Course Offers* (Trotman), published annually in the late spring, lists every course, together with the details of the A-level grades demanded by different universities.

John O'Leary (ed.), *The Times Good University Guide* (Collins) is also published annually in the late spring. Despite its relentless tendency to rank universities and departments, it contains a good deal of valuable information.

Klaus Boehm and Jenny Lees-Spalding, *The Student Book* (Trotman), is another annual, organised university by university.

Piers Dudgeon, *The Virgin Alternative Guide to British Universities* (Virgin Books), another annual, is arranged university by university: its distinctive feature is that it is based on students' comments. It is therefore especially useful as a guide to what it is like living in a range of university towns and cities.

T. Higgins, the Chief Executive of the Universities and Colleges Admissions Service, has written *How to Complete your UCAS Form for Entry into University and College* (Trotman), another annual publication.

Once you have a conditional place, you will almost certainly wish to contact the Student Loans Company: this is best done through their website, http://www.slc.co.uk Look too at the Government's guidance: http://www.dfes.gov.uk/studentsupport This site includes the official booklet *Financial Support for Higher Education Students in 2002/03*. G. Thomas, *Students' Money Matters* (Trotman, 2002) is a helpful general guide.

The University of Wolverhampton has developed a very useful website giving information about and links to British universities: http://www.scit.wlv.ac.uk/ukinfo/uk.map.html

All universities have their own webpages. The address usually ends in ac.uk – it is well worth exploring them. Look at the departmental webpages for the subject(s) you wish to study: you should find details of courses and profiles of lecturers.

There are many study guides written by professional educationalists. Derek Rowntree, *Learn How to Study* (1st edition 1970, Time Warner, 4th edition 1998), was one of the first and remains among the most useful. Stella Cottrell, *The Study Skills Handbook* (Palgrave, 1999) and Elsie Chambers and Andrew Northedge, *The Arts Good Study Guide* (Open University, 1997) are typical recent examples. My reservation is that such books are somewhat mechanical, and while they try to tell you how to study, they are less helpful in conveying what your lecturers are expecting from you. More helpful are the many books by Phil Race: for example, *How to Get a Good Degree* (Open University, 1999) and *How to Win as a Final Year Student* (Open University, 2000). Phil Race, *2000 Tips for Lecturers* (Kogan Page, 1999) is interesting for students too.

It is unusual for university lecturers who are not in departments of education to write books about studying. A long time ago, two outstanding scholars did. Under the pseudonym Bruce Truscot, Allison Peers, Professor of Spanish in the University of Liverpool, wrote two books about universities in the 1940s, most accessibly brought together in a single-volume Penguin, *Red Brick University* (1950), that can still often be found in second-hand bookshops. It remains an inspiring and idealistic evocation of what studying at university can and should be like. In his *First Steps at University* (Faber, 1947), he offered guidance to new students. Gilbert Highet, a classicist who moved from Oxford to Columbia University, New York, in the late 1930s, distilled his experiences in *The Art of Teaching* (1950; reprinted Vintage Books 1989). His book is intended in the first place for would-be teachers: but anyone who is studying will learn a great deal from Highet's wisdom too. Of course, these books are in many ways dated now, but over the years I have found it rewarding to re-read them: courses and examinations come and go, but the essence of learning is timeless.

Index